Transforming Health Care Scheduling and Access

Getting to Now

Committee on Optimizing Scheduling in Health Care

Gary Kaplan, Marianne Hamilton Lopez, and J. Michael McGinnis,
Editors

INSTITUTE OF MEDICINE
OF THE NATIONAL ACADEMIES

THE NATIONAL ACADEMIES PRESS
Washington, D.C.
www.nap.edu

THE NATIONAL ACADEMIES PRESS 500 Fifth Street, NW Washington, DC 20001

NOTICE: The project that is the subject of this report was approved by the Governing Board of the National Research Council, whose members are drawn from the councils of the National Academy of Sciences, the National Academy of Engineering, and the Institute of Medicine. The members of the committee responsible for the report were chosen for their special competences and with regard for appropriate balance.

This study was supported by Contract/Grant No. HHSP23337008 between the National Academy of Sciences and the Department of Veteran Affairs. Any opinions, findings, conclusions, or recommendations expressed in this publication are those of the author(s) and do not necessarily reflect the views of the organizations or agencies that provided support for the project.

International Standard Book Number 13:   978-0-309-33919-3
International Standard Book Number-10:   0-309-33919-7
Library of Congress Catalog Card Number: 2015947573

Additional copies of this report are available for sale from the National Academies Press, 500 Fifth Street, NW, Keck 360, Washington, DC 20001; (800) 624-6242 or (202) 334-3313; http://www.nap.edu.

For more information about the Institute of Medicine, visit the IOM home page at: www.iom.edu.

Copyright 2015 by the National Academy of Sciences. All rights reserved.

Printed in the United States of America

The serpent has been a symbol of long life, healing, and knowledge among almost all cultures and religions since the beginning of recorded history. The serpent adopted as a logotype by the Institute of Medicine is a relief carving from ancient Greece, now held by the Staatliche Museen in Berlin.

Suggested citation: IOM (Institute of Medicine). 2015. *Transforming health care scheduling and access: Getting to now.* Washington, DC: The National Academies Press.

*"Knowing is not enough; we must apply.
Willing is not enough; we must do."*
—Goethe

INSTITUTE OF MEDICINE
OF THE NATIONAL ACADEMIES

Advising the Nation. Improving Health.

THE NATIONAL ACADEMIES
Advisers to the Nation on Science, Engineering, and Medicine

The **National Academy of Sciences** is a private, nonprofit, self-perpetuating society of distinguished scholars engaged in scientific and engineering research, dedicated to the furtherance of science and technology and to their use for the general welfare. Upon the authority of the charter granted to it by the Congress in 1863, the Academy has a mandate that requires it to advise the federal government on scientific and technical matters. Dr. Ralph J. Cicerone is president of the National Academy of Sciences.

The **National Academy of Engineering** was established in 1964, under the charter of the National Academy of Sciences, as a parallel organization of outstanding engineers. It is autonomous in its administration and in the selection of its members, sharing with the National Academy of Sciences the responsibility for advising the federal government. The National Academy of Engineering also sponsors engineering programs aimed at meeting national needs, encourages education and research, and recognizes the superior achievements of engineers. Dr. C. D. Mote, Jr., is president of the National Academy of Engineering.

The **Institute of Medicine** was established in 1970 by the National Academy of Sciences to secure the services of eminent members of appropriate professions in the examination of policy matters pertaining to the health of the public. The Institute acts under the responsibility given to the National Academy of Sciences by its congressional charter to be an adviser to the federal government and, upon its own initiative, to identify issues of medical care, research, and education. Dr. Victor J. Dzau is president of the Institute of Medicine.

The **National Research Council** was organized by the National Academy of Sciences in 1916 to associate the broad community of science and technology with the Academy's purposes of furthering knowledge and advising the federal government. Functioning in accordance with general policies determined by the Academy, the Council has become the principal operating agency of both the National Academy of Sciences and the National Academy of Engineering in providing services to the government, the public, and the scientific and engineering communities. The Council is administered jointly by both Academies and the Institute of Medicine. Dr. Ralph J. Cicerone and Dr. C. D. Mote, Jr., are chair and vice chair, respectively, of the National Research Council.

www.national-academies.org

COMMITTEE ON OPTIMIZING SCHEDULING IN HEALTH CARE

GARY KAPLAN (*Chair*), Chairman and Chief Executive Officer, Virginia Mason Health System
JANA BAZZOLI, Vice President, Clinical Affairs, Cincinnati Children's Hospital Medical Center
JAMES C. BENNEYAN, Director, Healthcare Systems Engineering Institute, Northeastern University
JAMES CONWAY, Adjunct Faculty, Department of Health Policy and Management, Harvard School of Public Health
SUSAN DENTZER, Senior Policy Adviser, Robert Wood Johnson Foundation
EVA LEE, Professor and Director, Operations Research in Medicine and Health Care, School of Industrial and Systems Engineering, Georgia Institute of Technology
EUGENE LITVAK, President and Chief Executive Officer, Institute for Healthcare Optimization
MARK MURRAY, Mark Murray & Associates, LLC
THOMAS NOLAN, Senior Fellow, Institute for Healthcare Improvement
PETER PRONOVOST, Senior Vice President for Patient Safety & Quality, Johns Hopkins Schools of Medicine, Nursing, and Public Health
RONALD M. WYATT, Medical Director, Healthcare Improvement, The Joint Commission

IOM Staff

MARIANNE HAMILTON LOPEZ, Study Director (*from April 2015*)
MELINDA MORIN, Study Director (*until April 2015*)
ELIZABETH JOHNSTON, Senior Program Assistant
KATHERINE BURNS, Senior Program Assistant
MINA BAKHTIAR, Senior Program Assistant
LESLIE KWAN, Research Associate
GURU MADHAVAN, Senior Program Officer
J. MICHAEL McGINNIS, Senior Scholar and Executive Director, IOM Roundtable on Value & Science-Driven Health Care

Consultants

JOE ALPER, Science writer
REBECCA MORGAN, National Academies Library/Research Center
ROBERT POOL, Copyeditor

Reviewers

This report has been reviewed in draft form by individuals chosen for their diverse perspectives and technical expertise, in accordance with procedures approved by the National Research Council's Report Review Committee. The purpose of this independent review is to provide candid and critical comments that will assist the institution in making its published report as sound as possible and to ensure that the report meets institutional standards for objectivity, evidence, and responsiveness to the study charge. The review comments and draft manuscript remain confidential to protect the integrity of the deliberative process. We wish to thank the following individuals for their review of this report:

Karen S. Cook, Stanford University
Julie A. Freischlag, University of California, Davis, School of Medicine
Mark E. Frisse, Vanderbilt University
Christine Hunter, U.S. Office of Personnel Management
Beverley H. Johnson, Institute for Patient- and Family-Centered Care
Kenneth W. Kizer, University of California, Davis, School of Medicine
Charles E. Phelps, University of Rochester
Murray Ross, Kaiser Foundation Health Plan, Inc.
Vinod K. Sahney, Northeastern University
Katepalli R. Sreenivasan, New York University
Alfred F. Tallia, Rutgers University
Alan R. Washburn, U.S. Naval Postgraduate School

Although the reviewers listed above have provided many constructive comments and suggestions, they were not asked to endorse the conclusions or recommendations nor did they see the final draft of the report before its release. The review of this report was overseen by **Georges C. Benjamin,** American Public Health Association, and **Lawrence D. Brown,** University of Pennsylvania. Appointed by the National Research Council and the Institute of Medicine, they were responsible for making certain that an independent examination of this report was carried out in accordance with institutional procedures and that all review comments were carefully considered. Responsibility for the final content of this report rests entirely with the authoring committee and the institution.

Contents

	SUMMARY	1
1	**IMPROVING HEALTH CARE SCHEDULING**	7
	Introduction, 7	
	Context: VA Phoenix Health Center Crisis, 8	
	Context: National Issues in Access and Wait Times, 9	
	Committee Charge and Approach, 12	
2	**ISSUES IN ACCESS, SCHEDULING, AND WAIT TIMES**	17
	Terms and Patterns, 17	
	Scheduling Practices by Setting, 20	
	Factors in Scheduling Delays and Variability, 24	
	Benchmarking in the Absence of Standards, 30	
3	**SYSTEMS STRATEGIES FOR CONTINUOUS IMPROVEMENT**	33
	Lessons from Industrial Engineering Practices, 34	
	Systems Strategies for Health Care Scheduling and Access, 39	
	Challenges and Barriers, 47	
4	**BUILDING FROM BEST PRACTICES**	49
	Experiences in Service Excellence, 49	
	Commonalities in Success, 71	
	Capacity Implications, 73	

5	**GETTING TO NOW**	79

Capturing the Moment, 79
Committee Findings, 81
Committee Recommendations, 84
Accelerating Progress, 88

REFERENCES	91

APPENDIXES
A	Background Papers	107

    Open Access or Advanced Access Scheduling, 108
    Reengineering Flow Through the Primary Care Office, 112
    Reengineering Flow Through the Acute Care Delivery
       System, 115
    Framework for Active Patient Involvement in Access and
       Scheduling, 118
    References, 121

B	IOM Workshops in Brief	123

    Engineering Optimal Health Care Scheduling:
      Perspectives for the Nation, 124
    Engineering Optimal Health Care Scheduling:
      Perspectives for the Veterans Health Administration, 130

C	Committee Member Biographies	135

Summary

The Institute of Medicine (IOM) report *Crossing the Quality Chasm* (2001a) identified six fundamental aims for health care—that it be safe, effective, patient-centered, efficient, equitable, and timely. Of these fundamental aims, timeliness is in some ways the least well studied and understood. How can timely care be ensured in various health care settings, and what are some of the reasons that care is sometimes not timely?

The report presented here was developed by the IOM Committee on Optimizing Scheduling in Health Care to answer such questions. Although the study was prompted by attention to a high-profile crisis in a health center operated by the Veterans Health Administration of the Department of Veterans Affairs (VA/VHA), and it was commissioned by the VA, the report focuses broadly on the experiences and opportunities throughout the nation related to the scheduling of and access to health care. As a "fast track" Academy study, the report is limited as to the detail of practice considerations. It reviews what is currently known and experienced with respect to health care access, scheduling, and wait times nationally, and it offers preliminary observations about emerging best practices and promising strategies. The report concludes that opportunities exist to implement those practices and strategies (including virtually immediate engagement) and presents recommendations for needed approaches, policies, and leadership.

STUDY CHARGE AND APPROACH

Convened at the request of the VA/VHA, the committee was charged with the following tasks: (1) review the literature assessing the issues, pat-

> **BOX S-1**
> **Patient- and Family-Centered Care**
>
> Patient- and family-centered care is designed, with patient involvement, to ensure timely, convenient, well-coordinated engagement of a person's health and health care needs, preferences, and values; it includes explicit and partnered determination of patient goals and care options; and it requires ongoing assessment of the care match with patient goals.

terns, standards, challenges, and strategies for scheduling timely health care appointments; (2) characterize the variability in need profiles and the implications for the timing in scheduling protocols; (3) identify organizations with particular experience and expertise in demonstrating best practices for optimizing the timeliness of scheduling matched to patient need and avoiding unnecessary delays in delivery of needed health care; (4) consider mandates and guidance from relevant legislative processes, review wait time proposals from the VA/VHA Leading Access and Scheduling Initiative, and evaluate all evidence indicated above, along with input and comment from others in the field; (5) organize a public workshop of experts from relevant sectors to inform the committee on the evidence of best practices, their experience with acuity-specifics standards, and the issues to be considered in applying the standards in various health care settings; and (6) issue findings, conclusions, and recommendations for development, testing, and implementation of standards, and the continuous improvement of their application. Throughout its work, the committee has been guided by its view that health care must always be patient- and family-centered and implemented as a goal-oriented partnership (see Box S-1).

LEARNING FROM OTHER SECTORS

To address scheduling issues, the committee considered a number of established conceptual models and systems-based engineering approaches that have been applied in settings beyond health care. These approaches have enabled many organizations to improve quality, efficiency, safety, and customer experience. However, the success of these methods depends on their application simultaneously in every part of an interconnected system rather than being applied piecemeal to distinct individual processes, departments, or service lines. The notion of an integrated approach is a core concept for timely delivery of health care.

Systems strategies in health care delivery involve the use of scientific insights to illuminate the interdependencies of processes and elements and the effects of these interdependencies on health outcomes. The strategies also entail modeling system relationships, exploring design or policy changes, and optimizing overall performance to produce better health care delivery at lower cost and minimum waste. Most importantly, systems strategies emphasize the integration of all the systems and subsystems that influence health and the optimization of them as a whole. A systems approach to health care involves orienting the system on the needs and perspectives of the patient and family. It emphasizes an understanding of the system's supply and demand elements, developing a capacity for data analysis and measurement strategies, and incorporating evolving technologies. Finally, it relates to creating a culture of service excellence that empowers those on the front lines to experiment, identify limitations, and learn from trials.

LEARNING FROM EXPERIENCE AND BEST PRACTICES

Drawing not only on their expertise, but also on an extensive review of the literature, the comments at a public workshop held for open discussion of experiences and strategies, and an IOM discussion paper authored by leaders of five health care organizations that have implemented transformative changes, the committee identified innovative systems models that have been shown in limited settings to improve scheduling and wait time outcomes and to have either neutral or positive effects on the quality of care and patient experience. The examples presented reflect experiences in multiple specialties, care delivery settings, and business models and in organizations of various sizes and located in various geographical regions. They draw on process reengineering, resource reallocation, and behavioral change strategies. Applicable to ambulatory practices, hospitals, and rehabilitation facilities, such system-wide improvements can increase the likelihood that the right care will be delivered at the right time to every patient. Additionally, with further research into their efficacy, these models have the potential to be adopted more widely and to become the foundation for standards of care.

Specific approaches that have been successful in ambulatory care settings include scheduling strategy models and options that reframe supply and demand. Scheduling models include the advanced access model, also known as open access or same-day scheduling, in which a sizeable share of the day's appointments are reserved for patients desiring a same-day appointment (Murray and Berwick, 2003), and the smoothing flow scheduling model, which uses the operations management technique of smoothing flow to identify and quantify the types of variability in patient flow (demand) and the resources available to different patient groups (supply) (Litvak and

Fineberg, 2013). Options that reframe supply and demand include team-based workforce optimization strategies that increase provider capacity by assigning care tasks to appropriate members of the care team, delegating certain tasks to non-clinician team members (e.g., Brandenburg et al., 2015), and technology-based alternatives to in-person visits that address patient needs via phone, telemedicine, and/or mobile health units (Charles, 2000; IOM, 2000; Naylor and Imison, 2010).

Specific approaches that have been successful in inpatient and emergency care settings include the smoothing flow scheduling model, coordinated care models, and the use of systems and simulation models. Care coordination interventions can improve patient flow through hospitals by both improving output flow (i.e., assuring timely discharge) and preventing readmissions (Coleman et al., 2004, 2006). Systems models and techniques, such as Lean processes, can be used to identify and continuously monitor process inefficiencies causing the imbalances in patient demand and hospital capacity that lead to delays in patient flow and increased wait times (e.g., Cima et al., 2011; Lee et al., 2015). Simulation models can also be used as a planning tool to match hospital capacity to patient need (Everett, 2002; Jones and Evans, 2008; Kolker, 2008).

The committee presents case examples of organizations that have applied these systems strategies to improve scheduling and reduce wait times (see Chapter 4). The cases reflect experiences in multiple specialties, care delivery settings, and business models and in organizations of various sizes and geographical regions.

FINDINGS, BASIC ACCESS PRINCIPLES, AND RECOMMENDATIONS

Based on its review and discussions, the committee developed a set of findings and recommendations, which are presented throughout the report and described in detail in Chapter 5. The findings are summarized in Box S-2.

Additionally, throughout its work, the committee identified a number of commonalities among exemplary practices reflected in the literature and throughout the selected set of promising case examples. These commonalities, presented in Box S-3, represent a set of basic health care access principles for primary, specialty, and hospital and post-acute care scheduling, and also provide targets for expanded research and evaluation.

The committee recommendations, which are summarized in Box S-4, call out the need for leadership at both the national level and the level of each health care facility. Nationally, the committee emphasizes several key needs: the spread and implementation of the identified access principles; direct senior federal official collaborative leadership; tools and strategies

BOX S-2
Summary of Committee Findings

- **Variability:** Timeliness in providing access to health care varies widely.
- **Consequences:** Delays in access to health care have multiple consequences, including negative effects on health outcomes, patient satisfaction with care, health care utilization, and organizational reputation.
- **Contributors:** Delays in access to health care have multiple causes, including mismatched supply and demand, a provider-focused approach to scheduling, outmoded workforce and care supply models, priority-based queues, care complexity, reimbursement complexity, financial barriers, and geographic barriers.
- **Systems strategies:** Although not common practice, immediate engagement for patients is achievable through queue streamlining and related systems strategies to access and scheduling.
- **Supply and demand:** Continuous assessment, monitoring, and realigning of supply and demand are basic requirements for improving health care access.
- **Reframing:** Alternatives to in-office physician visits, including the use of non-physician clinicians and technology-mediated consultations, can often meet patient needs.
- **Standards:** Standardized measures and benchmarks for timely access to health care are needed for reliable assessment and improvement of health care scheduling.
- **Evidence:** Available evidence is very limited on which to provide setting-specific guidance on care timeliness.
- **Best practices:** Emerging best practices have improved health care access and scheduling in various locations and serve as promising bases for research, validation, and implementation.
- **Leadership:** Leadership at every level of the health care delivery system is essential to steward and sustain cultural and operational changes needed to reduce wait times.

BOX S-3
Basic Access Principles for All Settings

- **Supply–demand matching** through formal ongoing evaluation.
- **Immediate engagement** and exploration of need at time of inquiry.
- **Patient preference** on timing and nature of care invited at inquiry.
- **Need-tailored care** with reliable, acceptable alternatives to clinician visit.
- **Surge contingencies** in place to ensure timely accommodation of needs.
- **Continuous assessment** of changing circumstances in each care setting.

> **BOX S-4**
> **Summary of Committee Recommendations**
>
> **For National Leadership leading to:**
> 1. **Basic access principles** spread and implemented.
> 2. **Federal implementation initiatives** with multiple department collaboration.
> 3. **Systems strategies** broadly promoted in health care.
> 4. **Standards development** proposed, tested, and applied.
> 5. **Professional societies** leading application of systems approaches.
> 6. **Public and private payers** providing financial incentives and other tools.
>
> **For Health Care Facility Leadership leading to:**
> 7. **Front-line scheduling** practices anchored in the basic access principles.
> 8. **Governance commitment** to leadership on basic access principles.
> 9. **Patient and family participation** in designing and leading change.
> 10. **Continuous assessment** and adjustment at every care site.

developed to aid adoption of systems approaches to care scheduling and delivery; and coordinated efforts among key stakeholders to build the evidence base, test best practices, develop and implement standards, and create incentives for their application. In addition, leadership is necessary to ensure that in each health care setting, practices are anchored in the basic access principles; governance at the executive and board level is fully committed; and the perspectives of patients, families, and other stakeholder groups are included in planning, implementing, and evaluating institutional approaches to scheduling.

1

Improving Health Care Scheduling

INTRODUCTION

"How can we help you today?" Each of us would like to hear these words when seeking health care assistance for ourselves, for our families, or for others. It should not only be our wish, but our expectation. Health care that implements a "How can we help you today?" philosophy is care that is patient centered, takes full advantage of what has been learned about systems strategies for matching supply and demand, and is sustained by leadership committed to a culture of service excellence and continuous improvement. Care with this commitment is feasible and can be found in practice today.

Yet it is not common practice. In 2001, the Institute of Medicine (IOM) landmark report *Crossing the Quality Chasm* identified being timely as one of the six fundamental properties of high-quality health care—along with being safe, being effective, being patient-centered, being efficient, and being equitable (IOM, 2001a). Progress has been slow on many dimensions including programs to design, implement, and share innovative scheduling and wait time practices in order to advance the evidence base and create standards and accountability. The culture, technology, and financial incentives at work in health care have only recently begun to heighten awareness and attention to the issue that delays are often not the result of resource limitations but more commonly are the product of flawed approaches to the scheduling process and poor use of the full range of available resources.

Although prompted by attention to a high-profile crisis in a health center operated by the Veterans Health Administration of the Department of Veterans Affairs (VA/VHA), and commissioned by the VA, this report focuses broadly on the experiences and opportunities throughout the nation related to the scheduling of and access to health care. As a "fast track" Academy study, the report is limited as to the detail of practice considerations. It reviews what is currently known and experienced with respect to health care access, scheduling, and wait times nationally, offers preliminary observations about emerging best practices and promising strategies (including immediate engagement), concludes that opportunities exist to implement those practices and strategies, and presents recommendations for needed approaches, policies, and leadership.

CONTEXT: VA PHOENIX HEALTH CENTER CRISIS

In 2014, in response to allegations of mismanagement and fraudulent activity pertaining to health care scheduling, the VA/VHA Office of Inspector General conducted an audit of the VA Phoenix Health Care System. The interim report from that audit confirmed that the Phoenix Health Care System had been falsely reporting its scheduling queues and wait times. The audit found that 1,700 veterans in need of a primary care appointment had been left off the mandatory electronic waiting list (EWL) that was reported to VA/VHA leadership (VA, 2014b). Of greater concern was that the VA/VHA final report, *Review of Alleged Patient Deaths, Patient Wait Times, and Scheduling Practices at the Phoenix VA Health Care System*, identified 40 veterans who had died while on the EWL waiting for an appointment. While the report found that there is not enough evidence to conclude that the prolonged waits were the cause of these deaths, it documented a poor quality of care in the Phoenix system (VA, 2014e). The report further determined that in an attempt to meet the needs of both veterans and the clinicians employed by the VA/VHA, certain facilities had developed overly complicated scheduling processes that resulted in a high potential of creating confusion among scheduling clerks and frontline supervisors (VA, 2014e). The report concluded that inappropriate scheduling practices are a systemic problem across the entire system nationwide (VA, 2014e) and called for an end to arbitrary scheduling standards, for more transparency and accountability, and for more attention to be paid to the "corrosive culture" that led to the manipulation of data in the system (VA, 2014e).

In response to the findings of the audit, the VA/VHA deployed the Leading Access and Scheduling Initiative (LASI), a 90-day program to develop and deploy rapid changes across its entire system. LASI, which ended in September 30, 2014, resulted in the completion of 120 tasks and 60 deliverables, including the development of new performance management plans; the addition of primary care into the Patient-Centered Community Care for non-VA care program; a focus on transparency through the monthly publication of wait time data (VA, 2015a); and a number of activities and policies focused on schedulers, which included interviews in the field, a review of schedulers' grades to combat high turnover rates, and an educational campaign to standardize scheduling processes across the system.

In August 2014, the Veterans Access, Choice, and Accountability Act was enacted to provide funds for veterans to receive care in the private sector in the case of prolonged waits at VA/VHA facilities and also to provide funds for the hiring of a large number of health care providers and the acquisition of additional VA/VHA sites of care (VA, 2014f). The bill also required the VA/VHA to conduct an independent assessment of the hospital care and medical services furnished in its medical facilities as well as an independent assessment of access to those services.

In October 2014, the VA/VHA established the Veterans Choice Program in accordance with Section 101 of the Veterans Access, Choice, and Accountability Act. The Choice Program addresses the VA/VHA wait time goals in such a way that veterans enrolled in VA/VHA health care will be provided clinically appropriate VA/VHA care within 30 days of making a request for medical services. Veterans who cannot receive a scheduled appointment within the 30-day standard or who reside more than 40 miles from the closest VA/VHA medical facility are able to receive care from facilities outside the VA/VHA system (VA, 2014f).

CONTEXT: NATIONAL ISSUES IN ACCESS AND WAIT TIMES

The data on access and wait times in health care are limited, and there is a prominent deficiency in research, evidence-based standards, and metrics for assessing the prevalence and impact of these issues (Brandenburg et al., 2015; Leddy et al., 2003; Michael et al., 2013). However, the limited information suggests that similar scheduling challenges are found well beyond the VA/VHA and exist throughout the public and private sectors of the U.S. health care system. The available data show tremendous variability in wait times for health care appointments within and between specialties and within and between geographic areas.

Variability in Access and Wait Times

The VA/VHA data released in October 2014 indicated an average wait time of 43 days for new primary care appointments, with a range of 2 to 122 days across all VA/VHA facilities (VA, 2014c). Detailed data from a review of Massachusetts physicians revealed average wait times of 50 days for internal medicine and 39 days for family medicine appointments (MMS,

2013). A 2014 MerrittHawkins study of appointment wait times in 15 cities across the United States found significant variation per city and per specialty. For example, average wait times to see a cardiologist ranged from a high of 32 days in Washington, DC, to a low of 11 days in Atlanta (Merritt Hawkins, 2014). A Department of Defense review of the Military Health System's military treatment facilities and privately purchased health care services found that their average wait times for specialty care (12.4 days) and for non-emergency appointments (less than 24 hours) exceeded their internal standards, but there was variation across settings as well as a lack of comparable data with vendors because of alternative access measures (DoD, 2014).

Studies have also shown that children with coverage from Medicaid or the Children's Health Insurance Program are more likely than those with private insurance to be made to wait more than 1 month, even for serious medical problems (Bisgaier and Rhodes, 2011; Rhodes et al., 2014). Academic medical centers, which often function as safety net providers, are less likely to deny appointments to children with Medicaid or the Children's Health Insurance Program, but those children still experience significantly longer wait times compared to privately insured children (Bisgaier et al., 2012).

Most U.S. data on access to care come from surveys of patient experience, which refers to health care processes that patients can observe and participate in (Anhang Price et al., 2014). These include objective experiences such as wait times and subjective experiences such as trust in a provider, and provider and staff behavior such as provider–patient communication and continuity of care (Anhang Price et al., 2014). "Patient experience" is distinguished from "patient satisfaction," which provides an assessment of a particular care experience (Anhang Price et al., 2014).

The Consumer Assessment of Healthcare Providers and Systems (CAHPS) surveys are the principal surveys done on patient experiences with health care access and quality in the United States. CAHPS covers hospitals, health plans, and ambulatory care, among others. Managed by the Agency for Healthcare Research and Quality (AHRQ) through a public–private initiative, the CAHPS program develops standardized, tested, and publicly available measurement tools of patient experiences with health care access and quality, as well as standardized and tested methods for collecting and analyzing survey data (Lake et al., 2005). In the 2013 CAHPS clinician and group survey, 63 percent of U.S. adults reported getting appointments, care, and information for primary and secondary care when they needed it (AHRQ, 2015). In addition to CAHPS, a number of private vendors provide patient satisfaction instruments, including Arbor Associates, Inc., the Jackson Group, Press Ganey Associates, Inc., and Professional Research Consultants, Inc. (Urden, 2002).

Impact of Delays in Access, Scheduling, and Wait Times

Generally, positive patient care experiences are associated with greater adherence to recommended care, better clinical care and health care quality outcomes, and less health care utilization (Anhang Price et al., 2014). A patient's inability to obtain a timely health care appointment may result in various outcomes: the patient eventually seeing the desired health care providers, the patient obtaining health care elsewhere, the patient seeking an alternative form of care, or the patient not obtaining health care at all for the condition that led to the request for an appointment. In any of these cases, the condition may worsen, improve (with or without treatment elsewhere), or continue until treated. Thus, long wait times may be associated with poorer health outcomes and financial burden from seeking non-network care and possibly more distant health care. Long wait times may also cause frustration, inconvenience, suffering, and dissatisfaction with the health care system.

Impact on Health Care Outcomes

Extended wait times and delays for care have been shown to negatively affect morbidity, mortality, and the quality of life via a variety of health issues, including cancer (Christensen et al., 1997; Coates, 1999; Waaijera et al., 2003); heart disease (Cesena et al., 2004; Sobolev et al., 2006a,b, 2012, 2013); hip (Garbuz et al., 2006; Moja et al., 2012; Simunovic et al., 2010; Smektala et al., 2008) and knee problems (Desmeules et al., 2012; Hirvonen et al., 2007); spinal fractures (Braybrooke et al., 2007); and cataracts of the eye (Boisjoly et al., 2010; Conner-Spady et al., 2007; Hodge et al., 2007). The timely delivery of appropriate care has also been shown to reduce the mortality and morbidity associated with a variety of medical conditions, including kidney disease and mental health and addiction issues (Gallucci et al., 2005; Hoffman et al., 2011; Smart and Titus, 2011).

A study of wait times at VA facilities analyzed facility and individual-level data of veterans visiting geriatric outpatient clinics, finding that longer wait times for outpatient care led to small yet statistically significant decreases in health care use and were related to poorer health in elderly and vulnerable veteran populations (Prentice and Pizer, 2007). Mortality and other long-term and intermediate outcomes, including preventable hospitalizations and the maintenance of normal-range hemoglobin A1C levels in patients with diabetes, were worse for veterans seeking care at facilities with longer wait times compared to those treated at VA facilities with shorter wait times for appointments (Pizer and Prentice, 2011b).

Reducing wait times for mental health services is particularly critical, as evidence shows that the longer a patient has to wait for such services, the greater the likelihood that the patient will miss the appointment (Kehle et al., 2011; Pizer and Prentice, 2011a). Patients respond best to mental health services when they first realize that they have a problem (Kenter et al., 2013). However, because primary care providers can act as the gatekeepers for mental health care, patients face an even longer delay for mental health services because of the need to first get a primary care appointment.

Impact on Patient Experience and Health Care Utilization

Patient experience has also been shown to be associated with perceptions of the quality of clinical care (Schneider et al., 2001). A study of patient experiences in England found that although all elements of patient primary care experience (including access, care continuity, provider–patient communication, overall patient satisfaction, confidence and trust in doctor, and care planning) were associated with quality of care, straightforward initial access elements (e.g., the ability to get through on the telephone and to make appointments) were most strongly related with quality of care (Llanwarne et al., 2013).

The perception of longer wait times is also negatively associated with overall patient satisfaction (Thompson et al., 1996). A study of patients treated at a large U.S. academic medical center found that not only was overall satisfaction with the health care experience negatively affected by longer wait times, so too was the perception of the information, instructions, and treatment that the patients received from their health care providers (Bleustein et al., 2014).

Extended wait times are also associated with higher rates of appointment no-shows, as feelings of dissatisfaction and inconvenience discourage patients from attending a first appointment or returning for follow-up care (Meyer, 2001). In a survey of caregivers who brought children to an emergency department, difficulty getting needed care from a primary care provider, especially long wait times, was associated with increased non-urgent emergency department use, suggesting that delays that are unaddressed in one area of health care delivery may lead to delays in other parts of the health care system (Brousseau et al., 2004).

COMMITTEE CHARGE AND APPROACH

Scope of the Report

To address the challenges associated with access and scheduling of U.S. health care services, the VA/VHA requested the IOM to assess the range of experiences nationally and to identify existing standards and best practices. The aim was to make recommendations for improving performance throughout the nation on health care scheduling, access, and wait times, including, but not specific to, the VA/VHA (see Box 1-1).

Study Approach

As an accelerated study, the committee's task was addressed through one in-person meeting, which included a public workshop (a brief summary of which can be found in Appendix B), numerous conference calls, and directed staff work to assemble the evidence and identify exemplary practices. Primary attention was given in this work to gathering and examining the available evidence documenting demonstrated practices for improving access, scheduling, and wait times in health care; learning from presentations by representatives of organizations deemed to have developed beneficial strategies for productive change; and identifying principles for best practices based on the experiences of those organizations.

BOX 1-1
Statement of Task

An ad hoc committee will conduct a study and prepare a report directed at exploring appropriate access standards for the triage and scheduling of health care services for ambulatory and rehabilitative care settings to best match the acuity and nature of patient conditions. The committee will:

1. Review the literature assessing the issues, patterns, standards, challenges, and strategies for scheduling timely health care appointments.
2. Characterize the variability in need profiles and the implications for the timing in scheduling protocols.
3. Identify organizations with particular experience and expertise in demonstrating best practices for optimizing the timeliness of scheduling matched to patient need and avoiding unnecessary delays in delivery of needed health care.
4. Organize a public workshop of experts from relevant sectors to inform the committee on the evidence of best practices, their experience with acuity-specific standards, and the issues to be considered in applying the standards under various circumstances.
5. Issue findings, conclusions, and recommendations for development, testing, and implementation of standards and the continuous improvement of their application.

In the course of their work, the committee will consider mandates and guidance from relevant legislative processes, review VA/VHA wait time proposals from the Leading Access and Scheduling Initiative, and evaluate all evidence indicated above, along with input and comment from others in the field.

Evidence to guide decisions or actions comes in many forms—randomized controlled trials, observational studies, and expert opinion among scientists and health care professionals, as well as that among patients and their families (IOM, 2001b). Similarly, evidence is used for many purposes, including application to learn the effectiveness of an intervention under controlled circumstances, development of standards for assessing outcomes, and use in comparing the results of different approaches under different circumstances. The strongest form of evidence, well-designed systematic trials with carefully matched controls, is important when introducing a new treatment, but is often not available, or even necessarily appropriate in the assessment of health services with highly variable input elements. The fact that trial data are not available to assess approaches to scheduling and access is not in itself limiting, but the overall paucity of reliable study and experiential outcomes data from any source presents a challenge. The committee therefore relied on an extensive environmental scan. In its scan of access and scheduling in U.S. health care services, the committee looked at the VA/VHA, private and public providers, and other sectors. The scope of the committee's review covers first appointments and follow-up appointments for primary care, scheduling and wait times for hospital care, access to rehabilitation care, referrals to specialty care, and first appointments for mental health. The committee considered wait times to get an appointment and wait times within appointments and also ways to meet patient demand for health care other than in-person appointments.

The committee also enlisted the leaders of five institutions—Denver Health, Geisinger Health System, Kaiser Permanente, Seattle Children's Hospital, and ThedaCare—to report on the strategies, experiences, and results achieved in their respective systems (Brandenburg et al., 2015). The conceptual framework (see Figure 1-1) that was developed by the committee to guide its assessment of the factors shaping overall system performance identifies supply and demand assessments as the anchor inputs, plus major enabling or constraining influences from culture, management, patients—e.g., the leverage contributed by evidence- and theory-based systems engineering, enlightened management that creates a culture of change and improvement, and the extent of patient involvement.

According to the statement of task, the committee was to look at "ambulatory and rehabilitative care settings." Given the evolving and adapting continuum of care, and recognizing that ambulatory, rehabilitative, and acute care are interdependent, the committee chose to focus on scheduling and access issues within acute care as well as ambulatory and rehabilitative care. Its aim was therefore to generate a report that was meaningful and relevant to the entire health care system.

The statement of task also highlighted the Leading Access and Scheduling Initiative (LASI) for consideration and analysis, and the committee

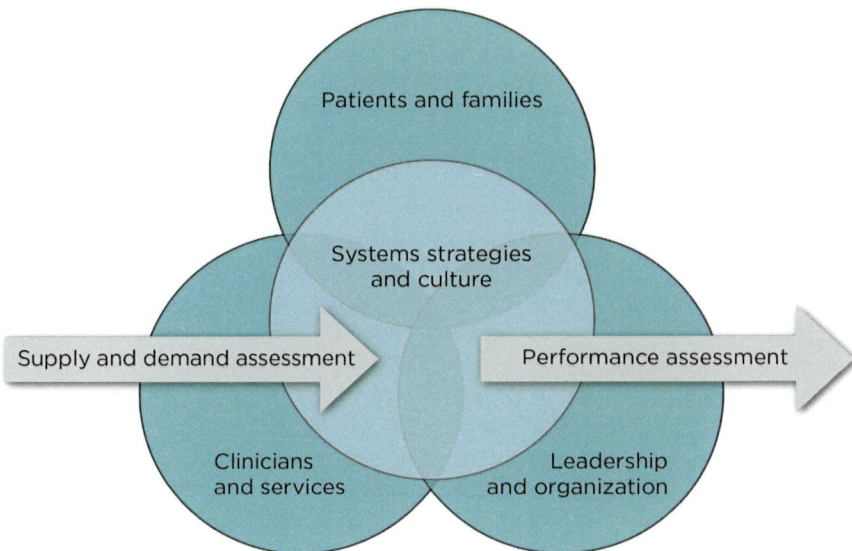

FIGURE 1-1 Framework for access and wait times transformation.

engaged in ongoing conversations with the VA/VHA about the intent and outcomes of the initiative. The information gathered during this communication is summarized above. However, in the absence of published information about LASI, the committee has not conducted additional analysis of LASI or offered findings or conclusions specific to the Initiative.

Structure of the Report

This report is intended to be useful to both the public and technical audiences and is composed of five chapters. Following this introduction and overview of the report's goals, Chapter 2 describes the current situation concerning challenges with access, scheduling, and wait times in health care. Chapter 3 describes systems strategies for continuous improvement and offers examples of how these strategies have been applied in other sectors. Chapter 4 describes a number of emerging best practices and alternative models for scheduling, including framing and operationalizing assessments of supply and demand. Finally, Chapter 5 presents the committee's findings and recommendations for transforming access and scheduling in health care.

A primary focus of the report is on primary care services, while laying the groundwork for improved access throughout other areas of the health care system. Primary care services form the core of the ambulatory health care system. Related scheduling approaches are key to success of initiation around accountable care organizations (ACOs) and medical homes. A foundational element of the committee's findings and recommendations is the centrality of orienting health care to the needs and perspectives of the patient and family (Berry et al., 2014). Patient-centered care has been described as an approach to the planning, delivery, and evaluation of health care that is respectful of and responsive to individual patient preferences, needs, and values (IOM, 2001a). With recent additional insights on the ability of meaningful patient engagement to improve the outcomes of care, the elements of patient-centered care have taken on additional clarity. Indeed, the committee views patient- and family-centered care not only to be designed with patient involvement to enable timely, convenient, well-coordinated engagement of a person's needs, preferences, and values but also to include explicit and partnered determination of patient goals and care options as well as ongoing assessment of the care match with patient goals (see Box 1-2). This is the perspective that has guided the committee's work throughout.

BOX 1-2
Patient- and Family-Centered Care

Patient- and family-centered care is designed, with patient involvement, to ensure timely, convenient, well-coordinated engagement of a person's health and health care needs, preferences, and values; it includes explicit and partnered determination of patient goals and care options; and it requires ongoing assessment of the care match with patient goals.

2

Issues in Access, Scheduling, and Wait Times

As background for the discussions in the report, this chapter defines some of the common terms and concepts from the area of health care access and scheduling, describes the scheduling practices most often seen in various health care settings, and identifies the basic factors that play a role in scheduling delays and variability.

TERMS AND PATTERNS

In the U.S. health care system, the three most commonly used scheduling techniques for both inpatient and outpatient services are block scheduling, modified block scheduling, and individual scheduling (NAE/IOM, 2005). In block scheduling, patients are scheduled within specific times throughout the day, such as morning or afternoon, and then seen on a first-come, first-served basis within that time frame. Modified block scheduling assigns a smaller number of patients to smaller segments of time throughout the day, such as hourly. Individual scheduling, the most commonly used scheduling technique in the country, occurs when a single patient is scheduled for a specific point in time, with the timing of the appointments determined according to the supply of care providers (NAE/IOM, 2005).

Although delays in care delivery are common—and unpleasant—occurrences in both public and private health care systems, there are few reliable data with which to determine the prevalence, degree, or nature of the problem. Even defining when a delay in seeing a preferred health care provider is inappropriate is not always straightforward.

There are a number of approaches for categorizing scheduling and wait time delays. They include approaches, such as the third next available appointment (TNA) for ambulatory care, defined as the average length of time in days between when a patient requests an appointment and the third next available appointment; boundary approaches, such as the 4-hour wait time target for emergency departments used in England and Australia (Hughes, 2010; IHI, 2014a,b; Jones and Schimanski, 2010; Weber et al., 2012); and the "office visit cycle time," defined as the time between a patient's arrival and departure times at a medical office, which can be used to separate productive time from waiting time. Each of these scheduling tools is focused on a delay in a different part of the patient care continuum. For example, TNA captures the delay in getting an appointment or service, whereas cycle time measures the delay at the appointment or service. They are different methods designed to capture delays in different processes. Patient views of acceptable wait times are also poorly captured in available scheduling assessment tools, and the measurement of these factors becomes costly and is often imprecise (Paterson et al., 2006). Some of the terms commonly used in discussions of patient scheduling are listed in Box 2-1.

BOX 2-1
Concepts and Terms in Patient Scheduling

Access includes contact with the health care system, availability of appropriate services, and the delivery of the services necessary to meet patient needs.

Actual wait time, a measure currently used by the U.S. Department of Veterans Affairs, is a retrospective time stamp that uses the date the appointment was created in the scheduling system or the date that the patient desired as the start date for the wait-time computation. The time of the completed appointment is used as the end point.

Advanced open access scheduling, also referred to as advanced access, open access, or same-day scheduling, offers a patient calling for an appointment the opportunity to be seen on the same day, preferably although not necessarily by the patient's customary clinician.

Block scheduling schedules patients within specific times throughout the day, such as morning or afternoon, and then they are seen on a first-come, first-served basis within that time frame.

Capacity, or supply is traditionally defined as the number of appointment slots available for a given period of time, such as 1 day, for all clinicians available during that period. Previous demand that has not yet been matched with appointments

BOX 2-1 Continued

shows itself as a backlog of work or a waiting list. The committee considers it important to view the term more broadly so that supply also entails resources that include labor, equipment, and any required physical environment for safe delivery. Demands can be met by supply elements that include face-to-face meetings, as well as other means, e.g., through a virtual care delivery infrastructure.

Demand traditionally refers to the total number of patient calls for appointments over a fixed period of time, such as 1 day, plus the number of walk-ins and the number of follow-up appointments generated by the physicians at a given practice site. Demand includes those patients that cannot be accommodated on a given day, as demand is independent of the limit of available appointments. The committee considers it important to view the term more broadly, so that demand not only covers the actual visits of patients but comprises all patients reporting problems daily.

Individual scheduling is the most commonly used scheduling technique in the United States, implemented through patient-by-patient scheduling for a specific point in time on a specific day, according to care provider availability in the care setting.

Modified block scheduling assigns a smaller number of patients to smaller segments of time throughout the day, such as hourly.

Office visit cycle time is a term applied to wait times that occur during an appointment. The office visit cycle time is generally measured from check-in to checkout for that appointment and can be broken down into various components of the visit. Each step in the cycle can be classified as either non-value-added time, such as time spent waiting for the next step in the visit, or value-added time, such as time spent with a care team member.

Supply–demand mismatch. An immediate cause of poor access to health care can be an imbalance between the demand for services and the available service capacity. Permanent imbalance, or mismatch, leads to a continued rise in delays until patients choose to seek medical care elsewhere. However, mismatch can also be impermanent, resulting from shifting variations in either supply or demand.

Third next available appointment (TNA) is a value determined by assessing appointment availability and is aimed at providing a reliable indication of the number of days that a patient has to wait to get an appointment (Murray and Berwick, 2003). Because the first and second available appointments are often the result of last-minute cancellations or other events, the third next available appointment best represents the performance of the appointment access system as a whole. TNA can serve as one metric to measure scheduling performance. It allows organizations to capture the TNA before and after an improvement is made.

Wait time to obtain an appointment within the health care system is a measurement of the access delay in the system and reflects the time differential between a patient's call or request for an appointment and an opening in a provider's schedule.

SCHEDULING PRACTICES BY SETTING

Health care scheduling practices vary by setting. Practices in the emergency room, for example, are different from those used by primary care physicians. This section provides an overview of the scheduling practices typically employed in various health care settings. It also discusses some of the issues that lead to delays and increased wait times.

Primary Care

Primary care providers typically serve a large and steady pool of regular patients, and relatively few new patients. The demand for primary care appointments usually has a predictable variation. There is higher demand for the first and last appointments of the day to accommodate work schedules and increased demand on Mondays and in the winter months. The variation in supply is less amenable to change, due to several factors, including competing priorities and responsibilities of the providers and workforce shortages. As a result of the recent Medicaid expansion and the number of patients who are now insured through state exchanges, a shortage has developed in the supply of primary care physicians in some areas of the country relative to the demand (Petterson et al., 2013). Although hiring additional physicians might seem to be the obvious solution to this shortage, given the financial constraints in today's health care sector, this is not a viable option for many health care organizations, and thus they need to find ways to make better use of the existing provider capacity.

No matter which of the three major scheduling techniques is used—block, modified block, and individual scheduling—the majority of scheduling decisions are generally based on predictions of patient need. Priority-based scheduling assigns different wait times to different patients according to assumptions made concerning the level of acuity or need associated with various conditions. For example, an individual with a history of congestive heart failure may be scheduled for follow-up visits at a periodic interval based on patient trends, rather than being given a schedule that reflects his or her actual needs, preferences, or circumstances. Priority-based scheduling creates multiple queues, each associated with a different wait time.

Specialty Care

Referrals and Transfers

The term *specialty care* describes any specialized practice that focuses on care for certain conditions or diagnostic or treatment approaches and primarily receives work as a consult, referral, or transfer (JHU, 2015).

Providing timely appointments for specialty care requires the same baseline measurements that are needed for primary care. Specialty care scheduling can be affected by a number of external factors that are not within the control of either the practice or the patient. These include delays caused by the requirement for insurance preauthorization, the need for additional diagnostic tests that are performed by third parties, and the referring provider not being co-located with the specialty care provider (Murray, 2002). For some conditions, it may be necessary for multiple specialists to coordinate their care, which introduces another level of variability that must be accommodated. An additional challenge for specialty care practices is responding to new patients with urgent needs while maintaining available appointments for returning patients.

Academic specialty practices experience a high degree of variability in providers' availability because the providers tend to have competing education, research, and clinical responsibilities. Although the natural variation in demand in an academic specialty setting is similar to what is seen in other types of settings, the higher degree of variability in supply can lead to challenges. These challenges are complicated by the presence of resident physicians, who are found in specialty care practices as well as other settings. Residents can increase the capacity of a clinic as their experience and training progress, but they can have frequent absences from the practice and require a more flexible model, with additional senior physician oversight. It is a challenge to achieve the competing goals of having patients see their own physicians, minimizing delay, and offering an educational environment for resident physicians. Any scheduling system used in specialty care must not only accommodate a clear definition of a care team, variable caseloads, and clinical times, it must also accommodate providers with substantially different experience levels.

Specialty Care: Providing Mental Health Services

With the implementation of the Affordable Care Act and the expansion of Medicaid, an increasing number of people are gaining access to treatment for mental health and addiction services because of the increased use of public and private insurance coverage. Yet timely access to these services is already a challenge for many Americans, especially veterans. And, given that both public and private health systems require patients to engage with primary care providers before allowing access to mental health care, the total wait times for such services are even longer. Because of the requirement to first see a primary care clinician, mental health patients waiting for transfer to facilities outside of the local health care system were found in one study to experience waits that averaged 15 hours (Weiss et al., 2012).

Emergency Care

Overcrowding, prolonged waiting times, patient care delays, and scarce resources are common in urban emergency medicine today (Yoon et al., 2003). Besides contributing to increased levels of patient frustration and anxiety, prolonged waiting times and protracted lengths of stay can also increase the proportion of patients who leave emergency departments without being seen by a physician (Johnson et al., 2009; Monzon et al., 2005). Emergency department wait times are often caused by hospital systems that require patients to remain in the emergency department while awaiting an opening elsewhere in the hospital (Hoot and Aronsky, 2008). Many hospitals in the United States have attempted to reduce emergency department wait times, but for various reasons their efforts often fail to produce sustainable results. One reason that many emergency department improvement programs do not produce long-lasting results is that the programs focus primarily on discrete processes, disregarding staff behaviors and overall system performance or organizational culture (Melon et al., 2013).

A factor considered as a critical contributor to emergency department overcrowding is patient boarding, or holding patients in the emergency department for observation, rather than discharging them or admitting them to the hospital (ACEP, 2008). Research has demonstrated a correlation between the length of stay in the emergency department and an increased risk of adverse events in patients who are subsequently admitted to the hospital (Guttmann et al., 2011). For example, as a relatively fixed resource for hospitals, bed availability becomes an increasing concern as occupancy increases. Using systems strategies, industrial models and optimization techniques, health care institutions can serve more patients treated in hospitals without increasing the number of actual beds, as is discussed in greater detail in Chapters 3 and 4.

Inpatient Care

Supply and demand are interconnected in a hospital process. There are entry points, exit points, and various steps or nodes involving patients within the system. Three types of delays can result: input delays, which are delays in access to a service, such as the delay for a bed, measured as the time between the decision to admit and the time the patient is actually admitted; throughput delay, or a delay that affects the length of time between a patient's admission and the time he or she is ready to be discharged from in the hospital; and output delay, a delay in the amount of time it takes to get a patient discharged from the hospital, such as a delay caused by a lack of availability of beds in a rehabilitation or extended-care facility (Hall, 2013).

Flow Coordination

Optimizing performance requires measuring the demand, capacity, and flow into and out of each node within the system, and system-wide assessments and adjustments are required to improve the overall collection of steps, including such steps as consolidating or removing processes in order to streamline patient service flow (Lee et al., 2015). The typical hospital includes individual departments and providers who work to meet or exceed patient care standards for their particular discipline. Although this can be an admirable goal, it can also lead to unintended inefficiencies, and it is preferable to rely on a whole-system model rather than a unit- or provider-centric model, which emphasizes performance in specific areas, often at the expense of interdepartmental or system-wide cooperation and coordination (IHI, 2003).

Transfer

Ideally, the movement of patients from admission through treatment and on to discharge should occur without significant delays. However, a department-centric or provider-centric environment focuses on the needs of individual areas, and one area's needs are not necessarily compatible with another area's priorities. For instance, nurses on a medical/surgical unit may not notify bed management that a bed has been vacated or may do so only after a substantial delay—because such notifications are not a high priority for the medical/surgery unit. This can lead to a situation in which there are vacant beds that could be occupied by patients who may be kept waiting somewhere else, including hallways or the emergency department.

Discharge

The discharge planning and placement processes require coordination and communication among personnel from different departments. The processes also need to have an agreed-upon care plan, and attention to various logistical challenges to ensure a patient's safety outside of the hospital setting, such as the arrangement of rehabilitative or in-home care. Ideally, discharge planning begins on the day of admission. Delayed discharges can cause problems because of their impact on hospital admissions and patient throughput. Delayed discharges may, for example, lead to a situation in which there are not enough available beds to meet incoming demand. Critical care units can find it difficult to move patients into step-down areas, which then directly affect admissions from the emergency department. Perioperative services can also experience backups while waiting for beds to become available in the post-anesthesia care unit (Jweinat et al., 2013).

Even under the best of circumstances, the discharge-planning process in hospitals is inherently complex. Patient-specific information (such as medical status and needs, patient and family preferences, and information about available community resources) must be gathered from many sources. Currently, Web-based discharge instructions have the potential to improve readmissions and transitional care (Bell et al., 2013). Poor-quality hospital discharge planning not only will affect the flow of patients within the hospital setting but also puts patients at risk for adverse events outside of the hospital, which in turn can lead to emergency department visits and hospital readmissions.

Rehabilitation Services

When returning to a home care setting is not an option, transfer to an inpatient rehabilitation facility (IRF), a skilled nursing facility (SNF), or a long-term care facility becomes necessary. The committee's review of the literature found scant information regarding IRF and SNF access, although reports are common of poorly informed family preferences leading to transfers and increased health care costs (Lamb et al., 2011).

IRFs provide hospital-level treatment with a focus on rehabilitation and face many of the same challenges related to access and wait times as acute care hospitals do. As with acute care hospitals, insurers have an influence on access to these facilities. In determining demand, it is important to have accurate measurements of admission trends, patient characteristics, and costs. At this time, the best practices for access to inpatient rehabilitation hospitals and skilled nursing facilities remain largely undocumented or validated and will require further development and evaluation.

FACTORS IN SCHEDULING DELAYS AND VARIABILITY

Some of the causes of prolonged wait times are inefficiencies in operation, in care coordination, and in health care organizational culture that result in flow disruption, the underuse of resources, and an imbalance between the demand of patients to be seen and the supply of providers, facilities, and alternative strategies to care for them at any given time (Mazzocato et al., 2010; Young and McClean, 2008). Organization-specific factors, including leadership and the resulting culture, can contribute to access difficulties and long wait times. The many complexities and process interdependencies of our health care system can complicate the challenge of balancing supply and demand.

Supply and Demand Issues

The most fundamental concept in scheduling is attention to the balance of supply and demand (Murray and Berwick, 2003). Unfortunately, most clinical settings do not take a broad enough view of the various options for either increasing supply or reducing demand, nor do they maintain the analytic capacity to observe and understand the dynamics involved (Murray and Berwick, 2003). As noted in Box 2-1, demand traditionally refers to the total number of patient calls for appointments over a fixed period of time, such as 1 day, plus the number of walk-ins and the number of follow-up appointments generated by the physicians at a given practice site. But many facilities define their supply simply in terms of the number of slots they have to fill on a given day or other period of time—that is, only in terms that relate to the availability of clinicians in that period of time. It is very unusual for a practice or clinic to keep a running record of the calls received, appointments made, wait-times, walk-ins, and no-shows, or to document how many queries could be handled by alternate clinicians, telemedicine, and electronic consults (Murray and Berwick, 2003).

Similarly, "supply" as traditionally defined in Box 2-1 is the number of appointment slots available for a given period of time, such as 1 day, for all clinicians available during that period. But often, for scheduling purposes, supply is viewed primarily as the slot availability for the clinician of record or requested by the caller, without consideration of (or the offering of) ways to augment the supply, such as other physicians and clinicians who are available; backup arrangements with other clinics for appropriate circumstances; and other sources, including digital and telephonic sources, that are available to meet callers' needs for information, referral, or advice. Without information of this sort, patterns of variability will be unobserved, alternatives will go untapped, and a supply–demand mismatch—which is often unnecessary—will be inevitable and chronic.

The committee considers it important to view the terms of supply and demand more broadly. Daily patient "demand" covers not only the actual visits of patients but also all contacts from patients reporting problems that day—each query requiring contacts from health care system resources to accommodate properly. Supply entails resources that include labor, equipment, and any required physical environment for safe delivery. Demands can be met via face-to-face setting or virtually. By reframing and expanding the notions of supply and demand, the relationship between a given care team and a patient panel could be expanded and redefined (Murray et al., 2007). Experience from various systems, including Kaiser Permanente and Group Health, suggest that at least 25 percent of patients calling in on a given day will not require an in-person visit but can have their needs addressed using methods such as telehealth (Darkins et al., 2008; Hsu et al.,

2012; Pearl, 2014). Regardless of the use of in-person appointments or alternatives, the supply and demand associated with any strategy that is adopted is dynamic and will become mismatched if not continuously measured, monitored, and readjusted as necessary.

The Current Provider-Focused Approach

The U.S. health care system is influenced by many competing priorities. Health care providers focus on providing care with autonomy and on receiving payment for that care. Providers have incentives to deliver higher paid services that can be supplied at low costs. Consumers seek accessible services and low out-of-pocket costs. Payers desire to select risks and limit costs. Because of these differences, the needs and priorities of different stakeholder groups are not always aligned (IOM, 2001a). The health care system currently reflects mainly the priorities of providers and organizations, which has resulted in a focus on traditional scheduling systems that have not been engineered to engage or satisfy patients but that instead are designed to fit a staff schedule that may be poorly aligned with patient perspectives or circumstances.

One emerging consequence is that, faced with the challenges of navigating the scheduling process for primary care, people often turn to other settings for their health care, such as retail health clinics (Zamosky, 2014). A 2013 survey of retail clinic users found that 58.6 percent of these patients used retail clinics because the hours were more convenient, and 55.9 percent because they could get care without an appointment (Tu and Boukus, 2013).

Outmoded Workforce Models

The Association of American Medical Colleges estimates that without an increased use of non-physician clinicians and staff, by 2025 the United States will have a shortage of 46,000-90,000 physicians (AAMC, 2014). Due to growth and replacement needs, the Bureau of Labor Statistics' Employment Projections 2012-2022 released in December 2013, projects 1.05 million job openings for registered nurses by 2022 (Bureau of Labor Statistics, 2013). The committee learned that efforts are under way, including within the VA/VHA, to identify and address the challenges of hiring and retaining core staff. For example, the LASI human resources workgroup's recommendations focused on such "areas as student loan repayment, the credentialing process, the pay system, hiring time frames, and nonmonetary incentives" (VA, 2014g).

Despite expected problems with physician understaffing, prevailing practices continue prioritizing physicians over other providers, and not using non-physician clinicians and other staff to their full capacity, such as in the provision of immunizations, pre-visit record screens, escorting patients to exam rooms (Gabow and Goodman, 2014; Toussaint and Berry, 2013), and by making use of other means of providing needed information and by offering remote site consultation. Such current workforce models will not be sufficient to meet future health care demands without other practice transformations (IOM, 2011).

As described in the IOM's *The Future of Nursing* report, transforming the health care system from one that is centered on provider convenience to one that is patient-centered will require re-conceptualizing the roles of all health care professionals, including physicians, nurses, allied health professionals, social workers, pharmacists, and other staff (IOM, 2011). As patient demands shift away from a focus on acute care to greater needs for primary care and especially chronic care management, the roles of health care professionals in the primary care setting need to be reevaluated in particular (IOM, 2011). Improving the performance of the primary care workforce will require practice redesigns. Small changes include such strategies as divesting from physicians tasks and responsibilities that can be performed by other members of the care team, while greater transformations through the enhanced role of nurses may include using nurses to facilitate care coordination, implement and manage informatics systems, act as health coaches, and serve as primary care providers themselves (IOM, 2011). Improving primary care capacity will also require making use of other means of delivering needed information and consultation (e.g., phone and Web-based video consultations). To that end, non-physician clinicians have the opportunity to play a greater role in the development, redesign, implementation, and delivery of such technology-based services (IOM, 2011).

Priority-Based Queues (Acuity Model)

As noted above, priority-based scheduling assigns different wait times to different patients according to assumptions made about the predicted need associated with different categories of conditions. This not only tends to limit the services provided and to require additional visits for other primary care services, but it also creates multiple categories—groups or queues—each with a wait time threshold established through assumptions about predicted clinical urgency associated with a given classification. Visits presumed to be routine or less acute are put off until a future date.

These estimated wait times reflect the best clinical judgment of providers, and the scheduling model was originally developed to help ensure patient safety and fairness. However, little formal evidence exists for the estimates of risk and need that should guide protocols for the timing of clinical appointments (Desalvo et al., 2000; Sirovich et al., 2008; Welch et al., 1999; Yasaitis et al., 2013). Furthermore, there are a number of challenges associated with the model. For example, urgent appointments placed through priority-based scheduling practices often address only one need per visit, which limits the opportunity for the care provider to meet multiple needs of the patient in a single visit. In addition, patients diverted to other settings for urgent care often want to follow up with their primary doctor later on, expanding a need for one visit into a need for multiple visits, and patients requiring visits deemed to be routine or less urgent can experience increased wait times (Murray and Berwick, 2003). Another challenge with the model is that—apart from truly immediate-need circumstances—the process of determining urgency in primary care using predictions of acuity that are based on a classification system is complex, difficult, and unreliable (Jennings, 2008).

Indeed, because of the limitations of the mathematical models used, priority-based scheduling models are likely to be unreliable any time that there is poor information on variation in demand or capacity. Because patients are sorted into multiple waiting queues, the provider supply is spread out, which introduces inefficiency and wasted time into the system. Queuing theory holds that the effect of variability on wait times will be more pronounced in a system with an increased number of queues (Saaty, 1961).

Care Complexity

As a result of health care innovation and the development of new treatments, patients are living longer with complex, chronic diseases, which has resulted in an aging population with increasing medical needs, involving physical and emotional conditions that require different types and amounts of health and related services (Bodenheimer et al., 2009). Providing appropriate, cost-effective care for a patient with multiple conditions can require coordination with multiple subspecialists, which can further complicate scheduling challenges. In the current provider-centered health care model, this requires the patient or the family to schedule multiple appointments, often on different days and in different locations, creating multiple opportunities for scheduling failures. Provider efforts are consistently challenged and strained by care complexity because of the limits of individual provider capacity (IOM, 2012).

Reimbursement Complexity

The ongoing changes in reimbursement have had a direct effect on patient access to health care. Medicaid patients, both adults and children, are limited in their access to health care, by virtue of limited acceptance among physicians of Medicaid payments. They also often experience poorer health outcomes than privately insured patients (Bisgaier and Rhodes, 2011; Hwang et al., 2005; Merrick et al., 2001; Wang et al., 2004). As Medicaid reimbursement rates have decreased, the number of providers refusing to accept Medicaid patients has increased (Tanne, 2010). As a result, Medicaid patients have an increasingly limited choice of providers from which to receive primary and specialty care.

Also contributing to prolonged wait times is the requirement for preapprovals imposed by payers. A preapproval is an authorization required by health insurance plans that patients must obtain before receiving certain services. Although intended as a cost-cutting measure to reduce unnecessary services, this requirement places an additional obstacle in the flow of care. A delay in any step of this process can lead to a prolonged wait time.

Financial Access

The Affordable Care Act has reduced the number of Americans without health insurance, but many in the United States still lack the financial means to pay for health care (KFF, 2015). In addition, as noted above, many practices, particularly specialty practices, do not accept patients who have public insurance. In one survey of wait times, the average rate of Medicaid acceptance by physicians across five specialties in 15 major metropolitan markets in 2013 was 45.7 percent, down from 55.4 percent in 2009, while in 2013 the average acceptance rate of Medicare patients was 76 percent (MerrittHawkins, 2014). Studies have also shown that children with Medicaid or Children's Health Insurance Program (CHIP) coverage are more likely than those with private insurance to be made to wait more than 1 month, even for serious medical problems (Bisgaier and Rhodes, 2011; Rhodes et al., 2014).

Geographic Access

The Veterans Access, Choice, and Accountability Act of 2014 offers a new national standard for geographic access for veterans and provides a choice to receive care in the private sector for those living more than 40 miles from the nearest VHA medical facility. The Department of Defense Military Health System has designated a standard of a 30-minute drive time for primary care appointments and a 60-minute drive time for specialty care appointments (DoD, 2014). For non-veterans receiving care in the private sector, access is typically determined by their insurance status, which requires patients to live within a specific geographic service area for enrollment and varies with each payer program. Care provided outside of the insurer network typically has higher patient copayments.

The Centers for Medicare & Medicaid Services (CMS) has also developed its own criteria for geographic access for applicants for its Medicare Advantage program. In a sampling of geographic areas, CMS analyzed the percentage of beneficiaries with access to a specialty type and varied travel time and travel distance to improve the system, which resulted in maximum time and distance criteria that vary by specialty type and geographic area. Providers within Medicare Advantage must demonstrate that 90 percent of their provider network meets the established time and distance requirements (CMS, 2015d).

Underlying these geographic and physical barriers to access is the reliance of the U.S. health care system on the office visit as the default model of care. Telehealth, or telemedicine, and the use of electronic information and technologies to support long-distance health care can be an alternative to an office visit and is discussed later in more detail.

BENCHMARKING IN THE ABSENCE OF STANDARDS

With all the different factors in play and with the lack of organizational attention to issues of prolonged wait times, the wide variation in the wait times is not surprising. As previously noted, according to access data publicly reported from VA facilities, statewide data from Massachusetts, and private-sector data from 15 metropolitan areas, there is significant national variability in wait times among care settings, among specialties, and over time (Council, 2014; MerrittHawkins, 2014; VA, 2014d). In addition to the significant variability in wait times among care settings, among specialties, and over time, there is a lack of national standards and benchmarks for appropriate wait times. Although references to timely care appear regularly in legislative proposals, a prevailing definition of timeliness has not yet emerged.

Instead, individual institutions are developing varied approaches and standards for appropriate wait times. For example, the Military Health System and the California State Department of Managed Health Care developed benchmarks for access and included the following (DoD, 2014):

- 30-minute drive time for primary care
- Specialty care appointments within 4 weeks
- Routine appointments within 1 week
- Urgent mental health care by a physician or non-physician clinician within 48 hours
- Non-urgent appointments with specialist physicians within 15 business days

- Non-urgent appointments with a non-physician clinician within 10 business days
- Urgent care appointments generally not to exceed 24 hours
- Emergency room access available 24 hours per day, 7 days per week
- 60-minute drive time for specialty care
- Office wait times not to exceed 30 minutes unless emergency care is being rendered to another patient

Benchmarks such as these have served as useful reference points at the practice level in various places. Yet, because they have not been validated for national use, they are of limited applicability. Though useful as examples, they can even carry the potential for unintended adverse consequences if applied arbitrarily and without consideration to local circumstances. The committee contends that although benchmarks can help an organization set a goal and move toward improvement, the benchmarks should be determined according to the unique capacity and demand of each organization and care site.

3

Systems Strategies for Continuous Improvement

The health care system is a complex collection of interacting elements, each of which affects the others in myriad ways. Effectively dealing with any health care system issue—especially as basic as scheduling and access—requires dealing with the various system dynamics in a coordinated way that takes into account how changes in one area will affect the functions in other areas. That is, it requires systems strategies and approaches.

Over the past 15 years, the Institute of Medicine (IOM) and the National Academy of Engineering (NAE), working both independently and collaboratively, have released publications calling attention to the growing concerns of patient safety, the quality of care delivered, and the cost of health care and also identifying potential solutions based on systems engineering approaches that have been widely adopted in technology and service industries (IOM, 2000, 2001a; IOM/NAE, 2005; Kaplan et al., 2013). For instance, the 2005 report *Building a Better Delivery System*, jointly published by the IOM and the NAE, observed that moving toward a functional system requires each participating element to recognize the interdependence of influences with all other units (IOM/NAE, 2005). More recently, a discussion paper described that a systems approach to health is "one that applies scientific insights to understand the elements that influence health outcomes, models the relationships between those elements, and alters design, processes, or policies based on the resultant knowledge in order to produce better health at lower cost" (Kaplan et al., 2013, p. 4).

Many other industries have faced issues similar to the scheduling and access issues faced today by the health care industry and have dealt successfully with them using systems strategies. In this chapter, the committee looks in particular to various industrial sectors for lessons on systems strategies that can be applied to health care. The chapter reviews the theory and practice of systems strategies as they have been applied to achieve continuous improvement in industry and how those strategies might be applied in health care, especially to improve scheduling and access.

LESSONS FROM INDUSTRIAL ENGINEERING PRACTICES

The tools of operations management, industrial engineering, and system approaches have been shown to be successful in increasing process gains and efficiencies (Brandenburg et al., 2015). In particular, a wide range of industries have employed systems-based engineering approaches to address scheduling issues, among other logistical challenges.

Systems-based engineering approaches have also been employed successfully by a number of health care organizations to improve quality, efficiency, safety, and customer experience, and these approaches have great potential for enabling further improvements in health care delivery (IOM/NAE, 2005). The success of these approaches will be dependent on achieving an overall integration across various health care domains and an application across interrelated systems rather than piecemeal testing across individual processes, departments, or service lines. By approaching improvement as a whole-system effort, a number of industries coordinate operations across multiple sites, coordinate the management of supplies, design usable and useful technologies, and provide consistent and reliable processes. With the right approach, it is likely that these principles can be applied to health care (Agwunobi and London, 2009).

Box 3-1 provides examples of systems strategies that originated in industry. The following sections further describe certain systems strategies that have been more widely applied to improve health care operations and performance. They are intended to illustrate the potential of systems approaches to improve health care scheduling and access.

Lean and Six Sigma

Lean is a value-creation and waste-reduction philosophy that was initially developed within the context of an automobile manufacturing system—the Toyota Production System—but that has now spread widely to service industries throughout the world. According to Lean philosophy, value is defined from the customer's orientation, meaning that valuable products and services are those that contribute to a customer's experience and needs and that can be provided to the customer at the right time and for the right price, all as defined by the customer (Womack et al., 2005). Correspondingly, waste is anything that does not add customer-defined

BOX 3-1
Systems Strategies

Deming Wheel or Plan-Do-Study-Act (PDSA) is a systematic series of steps for continuous improvement of a product or process. The cycle involves a "Plan" step, which involves identifying a goal and putting a plan into action; a "Do" step, in which the plan is implemented; the "Study" step, in which outcomes are monitored for areas for improvement; and the "Act" step which can be used to adjust the goal, to change methods, or to reformulate the theory.

Flow management is an operations research methodology involving the study of work flow and the introduction of dynamic control into processes.

Human factors engineering works to ensure the safety, effectiveness, and ease of use of various technological designs by explicitly taking into account human strengths and limitations in interactions with complex systems.

Lean is an integrated socio-technical systems approach and is derived from the Toyota Production System. The main objectives are to remove process burden, inconsistencies, and waste. In health care, the application of Lean has focused on the reduction of non-value-added activities and involves the identification of system features that create value and those that do not.

Queuing theory applies the mathematical study of waiting lines or queues in order to better design systems to predict or minimize queues. A variety of nonlinear optimization techniques (some based on the principles of statistical process control) have been put to work on different queuing applications, including challenges in telecommunications (phone call traffic), banking service management, vehicle routing, and even the express delivery of mail. Queuing theory has begun to be applied to multiple processes in health care involving groups or queues of patients.

Six Sigma is a quality management and continuous process improvement strategy. It improves efficiency by reducing variations in order to allow more capable and consistent products or processes. Six Sigma relies on the ability to obtain process and outcome data adhering to five principles: define, measure, analyze, improve, and control.

Statistical process control is a method of quality control that uses statistical methods to monitor and control a process to ensure that it operates at its full potential. This model focuses on the analysis of variation, the early detection of problems, and the reduction of waste and repeat work. In non-manufacturing applications, it has been used to identify bottlenecks in a system and reduce delays, including wait times.

Theory of constraints is a management paradigm used in complex systems to identify the most important limiting factors (constraints) in order to improve the performance of the system. Its application to health care is slowly increasing, and it has been used to increase capacity and revenue.

value to a product or service. The Lean approach relies on the continuous improvement of workflows, handoffs, and processes that function properly (Holweg, 2007; Ward and Sobek II, 2014). These workflows, handoffs, and processes required to produce and deliver a product to the customer constitute a "value stream." Value stream mapping is an important tool of the Lean approach. It documents in great detail every step of each process in a flow diagram, and it provides a visual portrayal of the many intricate details, sequences of workflow, and interdependencies in a process, which makes it possible to more easily identify problems and inefficiencies. As such, value stream mapping facilitates identifying activities that contribute value or waste or that are in need of improvement.

Lean is well suited for making changes to groups of processes rather than for making small, discrete changes to a single process, and in health care it has typically been used in large settings like hospitals. Lean has been used to improve both operational processes and clinical care, with applications ranging from improving insurance claims processing and improving patient safety processes to establishing a standardized set of instruments for surgical procedures (Varkey et al., 2007; Womack et al., 2005). The Lean philosophy has also been applied to health care delivery to reduce wasteful activities such as delays, errors, and the provision of unnecessary, inappropriate, or redundant procedures or care (Young et al., 2004). This capability is particularly promising for improving scheduling and access in health care.

Another business management and continuous process improvement strategy that has been widely adopted across service industries is Six Sigma.[1] Originally developed in Motorola, the approach is rooted in statistical process control and is aimed at dramatically reducing errors and variation. The term Six Sigma refers to achieving a level of quality so that there are no more than 3.4 defects per million parts produced. The Six Sigma approach has five phases, identified as define, measure, analyze, improve, and control (Harry, 1998). After its development at Motorola, the method was quickly adopted by industries ranging from hospitality to finance. Like Lean, Six Sigma has been applied to improve health care operations and delivery, with applications ranging from insurance claims processing to reducing medication errors and improving patient flow through laboratory services (Kwak

---

[1] Six Sigma is a data-oriented practice that originated in the manufacturing sector with interests to dramatically reduce defects from a production process. The approach has been applied both from a technical sense and a conceptual sense across various fields of practice. Sigma in statistics denotes deviation from the standard. At a one sigma level, the process may produce 691,462 defects per million opportunities (DPMO), and at three sigma, approximately 66,807 DPMO. At a six sigma, the process produces only 3.4 DPMO with a total yield of 99.99966 percent. Beyond the technical approach, Six Sigma concepts have also been used as a generic root cause analysis to detect and rectify defects toward reaching strategic goals (Evans and Lindsay, 2015; Schroeder et al., 2008).

and Anbari, 2006). Lean and Six Sigma are often combined when a key goal is to reduce waste and errors (Gayed et al., 2013; Paccagnella et al., 2012).

Crew Resource Management

In response to a series of airplane crashes caused by human error, the airline industry developed Crew Resource Management (CRM), a system for job training and information sharing (Cooper et al., 1980). Since CRM has been adopted industry-wide, pilots, flight attendants, and ground crews proactively communicate and work cooperatively, using tools such as checklists and dedicated listening techniques that have greatly reduced the hazards of commercial air travel. In the United States, the rate of fatal commercial aviation accidents fell from approximately seven per million departures in the mid-1970s to around two per million departures in the mid-1980s (Savage, 2013). Since 2005, the rate of fatal aviation accidents has remained under one per million departures (Savage, 2013).

The value of using checklists is already beginning to be realized in health care (Pronovost et al., 2006). Most notably, the checklists used in preoperative team briefings to improve communication among surgical team members are indicative of the potential that checklists have to improve patient safety (e.g., reduce complications from surgery) and reduce mortality in general (Borchard et al., 2012; Haynes et al., 2009; Lingard et al., 2008; Neily et al., 2010; Weiser et al., 2010).

Customer Segmentation and Cluster Analysis

Service and e-commerce industries commonly use customer segmentation and cluster analysis—modeling and marketing techniques that group potential customers by characteristics and preferences in order to appropriately tailor products and services. For example, Amazon looks to previous purchases and browsing behaviors to profile and segment its customer base (Chen, 2001). Netflix uses data mining and machine learning techniques to cluster user behavior data, like product ratings and page views, as well as product features such as movie genres and cast members to recommend new movies that customers are likely to rate highly (Bell and Koren, 2007). Values, Attitudes, and Lifestyles (VALS) is a commonly used research methodology for customer segmentation. Developed in 1978 by social scientist Arnold Mitchell at Stanford University, VALS breaks down customer motivations and resources and remains an integral aspect of large company marketing strategies to this day (Yankelovich and Meer, 2006).

One setting in which patient segmentation has been applied in health care is the use of patient streams in emergency departments. Patient streaming is the use of set care processes (or streams) to which patients are assigned upon triage; a subset of streaming is fast track, in which lower acuity patients are assigned to a fast track stream (Oredsson et al., 2011). Evidence on patient streaming is limited, although studies suggest that use of severity-based fast track in emergency departments can be effective at reducing waiting times, length of stay, and the number of emergency department patients who leave before being seen, while also increasing patient satisfaction (Oredsson et al., 2011). These limited uses of patient segmentation therefore focus on patient characteristics like severity, urgency, and likelihood of adherence, but less information is known about the potential of segmentation by patient-driven characteristics, such as preferences and values (Liu and Chen, 2009).

Deming Wheel or Plan-Do-Study-Act (PDSA) Cycle

Deming Wheel or Plan-Do-Study-Act (PDSA) cycle is the scientific method used for action-oriented learning (Taylor et al., 2013). The PDSA cycle is a series of steps for gaining insight of the control and continuous improvement of a product or process. The cycle involves a "Plan" step, which involves identifying a goal and putting a plan into action; a "Do" step, in which the plan is implemented; the "Study" step, in which outcomes are monitored for areas for improvement; and the "Act" step, which can be used to adjust the goal, to change methods, or to reformulate the theory (Taylor et al., 2013). The PDSA steps are repeated as part of a cycle of continuous improvement. The Institute for Healthcare Improvement (IHI) Model for Improvement focuses on setting aims and teambuilding to achieve change. The model uses a PDSA cycle to test a proposed change in the actual work setting so that changes are rapidly deployed and disseminated, and it is best suited for a continuous process improvement initiative that requires a gradual, incremental, and sustained approach to process improvement changes that are not undermined by excessive detail or unknowns (Huges, 2008).

Common to each of these practice areas is the integrative dimension. A systems approach emphasizes integration of all the systems and subsystems involved in a particular outcome. Adjusting each component of a system separately does not lead to an overall improved system. The fundamental elements of a systems approach to health care scheduling and access and the potential of systems strategies to improve scheduling and access are discussed in the next section.

SYSTEMS STRATEGIES FOR HEALTH CARE SCHEDULING AND ACCESS

The committee's view is that by using systems strategies, the organizational capacity or performance of health care system can be dramatically improved. Essential to the process is an understanding of the many system complexities and interdependencies. Although different resources and talents may require near-term additions, the aim is for better performance with fewer resources per service provided. Additional personnel and financial investment are generally not essential to achieving significant improvements in capacity over time (Lee et al., 2015b; Litvak, 2015). Figure 3-1 depicts the key principles of capacity management and their operational applications at Cincinnati Children's Hospital Medical Center (CCHMC), which was able to significantly improve productivity. CCHMC includes an administrative group that oversees the capacity of the system and evaluates and designs strategies to match changing demand. Using techniques of production planning from industry, CCHMC combines management and staff to set operating rules, monitor supply, measure delays, and make decisions about how shared resources are deployed.

Initiative	Operations Possibilities
Management of Variability	Identify Patient Streams – Inpatient/Outpatient Stream management, supply chain, best practices
Predictable Care Delivery	Best Practices, Identification of ALOS and outliers Physician Practice Models, Metrics of care delivery
Capacity Prediction	Integration of simulation modeling and planning Plan for flow vs reactive flow to plan
Capacity Management	Simulation to design for unit use and patient placement
Optimization of Flow Delivery	Placement initiatives – D:C Matching plans D/C planning, Home Care, Parent Initiatives
Flow:Safety Matching	Demand:Capacity Matching, SSE/Near Miss events related to placement, flow *watch-points* of care

FIGURE 3-1 System capacity management roadmap.
NOTE: ALOS = average length of stay; D:C = demand to capacity; D/C = discharge; SSE = serious safety event.
SOURCE: Cincinnati Children's Hospital Medical Center.

Defining Focus, Identifying the Components, and Building the Capacity

The basic building blocks of applying a systems approach to health care scheduling include fixing the system orientation on the needs and perspectives of the patient and family; understanding the supply and demand elements; creating capacity for data analysis and measurement strategies; incorporating evolving technologies; creating a culture of service excellence; assuring accountability and transparency; committing to continuous process improvement; and developing a supportive culture and organizational leadership that empowers those on the front lines to experiment, identify the limitations, and learn from those trials. These elements of health care scheduling from a systems perspective are discussed in more detail in the remainder of the chapter. With additional research and testing, these elements of health care scheduling could potentially serve as general principles for improving primary, secondary, hospital, and post-acute care. Although these elements are discussed independently, the central premise lies in their interplay; health care organizations are not discretely separated environments or services, but they are complex groups of processes, personnel, and incentives. These core access principles are therefore interdependent.

Fixing the System Orientation on the Patient and Family

Systems approaches focus on improving products and services placing customer needs at the forefront. When translating these approaches from the commercial setting to health care, however, identifying the "customer" has been challenging, because customers of health care may include patients and their families, providers (e.g., physicians), hospitals, and payers (e.g., the government, insurers, taxpayers) (Womack et al., 2005; Young et al., 2004). For example, improving scheduling includes reducing wasted time for both providers and patients. However, as described in Chapter 1, the committee's "How can we help you today?" philosophy for health care scheduling and access is driven by meeting patient need. Fundamentally, the patient is the primary focus for the organization and delivery of health care services and products. The activities to improve health care scheduling and access should aim to improve the patient experience and meet patients' needs as the foundational tenet of a patient-centered health care system (Bergeson and Dean, 2006).

The committee developed a framework for patient and family engagement for care, scheduling, delivery, and follow-up (see Figure 3-2). The framework uses a value-stream map for an office visit documenting the patient's care through the visit from the perspective of the patient as well as the attributes of an ideal system. As shown in Figure 3-2, each step encountered by the patient during a visit is documented, including the many

1. **Query:** Patient presents health question
   - Patient can access system 24/7; system responds immediately
   - Patient's concerns are respected

2. **Engage:** There is a collaborative process to answer question
   - Communication is provided in an understandable and convenient way

3. **Schedule:** Patient can easily/quickly schedule consultation
   - Patient can schedule care 24/7 and can do so online
   - Rescheduling is easy and readily available
   - New appointments can be synchronized with existing ones

4. **Prepare:** Patient can make preparations in the interim
   - Needed prior approvals and forms are obtained automatically
   - Needed lab tests are arranged and scheduled automatically
   - New appointments can be synchronized with existing ones

5. **Meet:** Patient has encounter with health care provider
   - Encounter takes place in person, online or by telemedicine
   - Encounter takes place on time; patient is given alternatives to waiting (when delays occur)
   - Staff is respectful and courteous; exam space private and comfortable
   - Team goes to patient

6. **Act:** The patient and provider take follow-up action
   - Understandable visit summary is provided on patient portal and hard copy
   - Team uses teach-back to ensure patient understands critical information
   - Rest of care team fully informed about visit
   - Prescriptions are e-prescribed

7. **Communicate:** Patient has ongoing care from care team
   - Any follow-up appointments are scheduled
   - Care team checks in to answer questions or ensure follow-up care

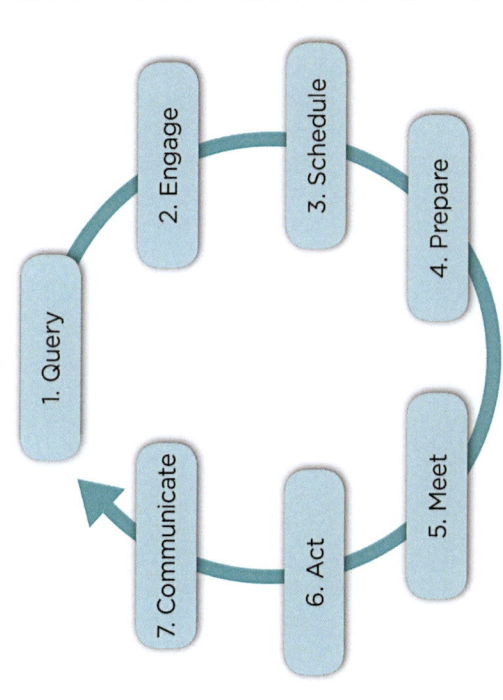

FIGURE 3-2 Framework for patient and family engagement: Care scheduling, delivery, and follow-up.

individual steps that are not intentional yet are part of the typical process. This is followed by a determination of whether each step actually improves the patient visit in some way. Following such an analysis, steps that are not valuable to patients are eliminated.

Institutions that have involved patients in systems redesign activities have reported positive results from such efforts, including improvements in patient safety with reductions in medical errors and improved satisfaction among patients and health care providers (Davis et al., 2007; Graban, 2012; Longtin et al., 2010; Toussaint and Berry, 2013). It is important to note that while involving patients in systematic improvement efforts has shown to have positive impacts, many unresolved questions remain that deserve additional study beyond the scope of this report, about who should be involved and how to ensure that patient involvement has more than a token impact (Armstrong et al., 2013; Martin and Finn, 2011).

Balancing Supply and Demand

Balancing supply and demand at each step along the care continuum is essential for an efficient and effective health care system (Hall, 2012). Poorly performing systems often contain design flaws, due to an excessive focus on the supply side and not on the demand side (Grumbach, 2009). Inherent capacity, for example, the number of appointment slots available, refers to the amount of demand each system can tolerate without creating a mismatch (Anupindi et al., 2005). Imbalance of patient demand and provider supply creates delays and increases wait times. If demand equals capacity, no delay exists. However, variations in either supply or demand can cause temporary mismatches that may increase wait times. Systems strategies require ongoing assessment of supply, demand, work flow, and patient flow, adjusting capacity across days and services, and continuous improvement.

In ambulatory primary care settings, temporary supply deficiencies can often be overcome by flexing or adjusting supply to keep up with demand, by temporarily increasing office hours, or adding another provider. In the primary care setting, capacity is determined by the number of providers, their hours worked, and the total number of patients seen each day. Capacity in the primary care setting is maximized through balanced panel sizes, a commitment to continuity, an appointment decision logic that directs patients to their own provider rather than the first open slot, and fully developed contingency plans that can address demand or supply variations. Optimal performance in this setting is currently measured as a TNA of zero for each patient's regular primary care provider (Murray and Berwick, 2003).

In the specialty care setting, capacity is affected by competing demands, with provider presence having the greatest impact. Capacity, therefore, is influenced by the frequency of which specialists are absent from the office. A key factor in this setting is that new patients can be a more critical part of a specialty care practice, which necessitates the creation of specific provisions for accommodating both the high volume of work associated with a new patient and the large number of returning appointments that must also be available. As a result, capability in specialty care settings is often determined by the volume of new patients. Whereas primary care systems are designed for providers to act and function as independent units, specialty care systems are designed to function as units of interchangeable providers. In that respect, the design elements that can enhance the capability of specialty care practices include a logic that offers appointment to the first available new patient slot for any provider among the entire set of interchangeable providers, a commitment to continuity once a new visit is completed, and fully developed contingency plans to address demand or supply variation.

Creating the Infrastructure for Data Analysis and Measurement

A health information technology infrastructure, including the creation and implementation of electronic health records (EHRs), is designed to generate data that will enhance the quality of patient care. Better use of the capacity to track patient flow through the health care system is a logical application, with potential to improve understanding of patterns of patient demand, provider supply, and bottlenecks to patient flow, and, as a result, improved revenues, hospital performance, and patient care (Devaraj et al., 2013). Indeed, implementing and sustaining systems strategies to improve scheduling in health care requires real-time performance data. However, most data systems do not currently include operational (e.g., wait times) data.

New systems should ensure that operational data integrate seamlessly with existing processes, and also that operational data are interoperable to enable communication and data exchange with other health care organizations to allow for the creation of a nationwide health information network. To facilitate operational data interoperability and the assessment of comparative performance across various care settings, practices, and circumstances, data need to be collected in a standardized, consistent, and sustained manner. Several aspects of health care scheduling and access that should be measured and for which standards should be identified include: patient and family experience and satisfaction; care match with patient goals; scheduling practices, patterns, and wait times; cycle times, provision and performance experience for alternative care models (e.g., telehealth and other remote site services); and effective care continuity.

The most important standards-setting organization is the individual health care organization itself. Therefore, each health care organization will need to define measures to assess its commitment to creating a standard of care and performance culture that supports timely scheduling and access. However, to define these measures and identify appropriate standards for scheduling and wait times, for which there are no existing national standards or benchmarks, health care organizations will need reliable information, tools, and assistance from various national organizations with the requisite expertise in developing and testing standards. Furthermore, given the need for flexibility of measures to assess the goals and performance of individual organizations, developing a measurement infrastructure for operational data will require inter-organization coordination to ensure harmony of reporting instruments and reference resources across the nation.

Once standards and benchmarks for access and wait times and corresponding patient experience measures have been identified, such performance data should be accompanied by analytic tools that can continuously monitor current conditions, including the scheduling measures of supply and demand. Health care organizations, again with the assistance of national organizations with expertise in developing and testing standards, will also need to develop, test, and implement standardized approaches to analyzing operational data.

Incorporating Evolving Technologies in Health Care

Various technologies are emerging with strong potential to improve real-time access to care, with the promise of totally new ways of scheduling and delivering care and gathering information on its utility. Use of digital and social media, telemedicine and telehealth, remote monitoring, and related evolving technologies are also well suited for deployment in health care practices. Still, their uptake has been relatively limited to date, for such reasons as unfamiliarity, system mismatch, and absence of reimbursement. Quickening use of these tools in health and health care will require receptivity to innovation, novel partnerships, and collaborative information and experience gathering. Health care providers are slowly developing new skills and integrating novel uses of technology into their organizations. The Health Information Technology for Economic and Clinical Health (HITECH) Act has accelerated use of EHRs, including more use of patient portals to aid information exchange with hospitals and other providers within the same system (Adler-Milstein et al., 2011).

Expanding EHR capabilities foster substantially enhanced insights into the continuum of patient and family experience, documentation of different patient information and preferences, analysis of data trends and predictions, and the integration of real-time monitoring of operations. To effectively use technology requires trust in the tools, adequate education of its potential, and a greater service commitment from the technology sector both for those working within the health care arena and for the patients.

The benefit to both parties must be demonstrated and reinforced, in part through organizational leadership and through individual providers. As practice efficiency and reimbursement changes occur, additional payment reform may be needed (Howley et al., 2015).

Some patients are beginning to take control of their own scheduling as they are gaining access to their medical information. This is not an entirely novel practice, having been implemented in high-performing, early-adopting organizations and practices. The changes described above point to a time when all clinical information is instantly available throughout the nation; when the EHR reveals not only past and scheduled appointments but also the sequence of referrals to specialists and resulting input, and patient preferences are documented throughout the scheduling process.

Creating a Culture of Service Excellence and Leadership Stewarding Change

Implementing systems approaches in health care, including strategies to address scheduling and access issues, requires changes not only in operational processes but also a fundamental shift in thinking. All members of a health care organization must transition from the siloed, independent, and fragmented mentality of traditional health care culture to a culture of service excellence, an integrated approach with shared accountability in which physicians, employees, and patients treat one another with respect and as partners, and patient satisfaction and employee engagement are high.

Organizational and cultural changes needed to support the implementation of systems approaches will require new competencies and participation from all members of a health care organization's senior management team (Trastek et al., 2014). Moreover, because changing an organization's culture often happens slowly, leadership and governing bodies at each level of the health care delivery sites are important in order to drive culture change and manage ongoing process changes (Kabcenell and Luther, 2012). Leadership is also important to establish and model standards of behavior for all employees and to establish educational opportunities to help employees learn the new behaviors. Finally, leadership and governing bodies' commitment at each level of the health care delivery sites is essential to promote transparency, accountability, successful adoption of technology, and continuous process improvement through ongoing monitoring of performance and process to avoid backsliding.

Transparency and Accountability

Transparency on performance draws data from disparate sources and delivers them to those at the front lines of care, including both patients and providers. Transparency helps employees understand the relevance and impact of change, informs and motivates their actions (on access, scheduling, or the other important elements of the care process), and helps organizations track the progress that they are making toward the desired new culture. Applied to scheduling and access, transparency about operational processes and their effectiveness can facilitate identification of delays and their causes, and also the progress made to reduce those delays. Finally, transparency facilitates messaging that creates organizational consistency—when everyone hears the same message from their leaders, they are motivated to respond in similar ways, and this behavior change can reinforce culture change.

The corollary requirement to transparency is accountability, or shared responsibility for organizational performance, to ensure that change is sustained in an organization (Blumenthal and Kilo, 1998). Accountability for all persons promotes accountability at all levels of an organization (O'Hagan and Persaud, 2009). Whereas the fragmented, independent nature of traditional culture may lead to lack of accountability or individual blame, in a culture of service excellence that takes a systems approach to improvement, accountability ensures that problems are analyzed in a holistic manner. Applied to scheduling and access, accountability may help ensure that delays in patient flow are addressed by all relevant stakeholders across the care continuum, rather than with independent, piecemeal process changes.

Continuous Process Improvement

A defining characteristic of modern health care is the rapidly accelerating increase in information that is available to assist with the delivery of care and system management. This places a high premium on the need for systems to effectively manage the flow of information, but it also requires a commitment by the organization to build and incorporate processes for continuous learning, knowledge sharing, and innovative change. Such characteristics are shared by health systems, including Denver Health, Geisinger Health System, Kaiser Permanente, Seattle Children's Hospital, ThedaCare, and Virginia Mason Hospital and Medical Center, who have adopted methods of continuous improvement such as Lean, the IHI Model for Improvement, and Six Sigma to empower teams to question how things are done and recommend operational changes to improve efficiency (Brandenburg et al., 2015).

Continuous process improvement uses data for ongoing improvement of the quality of a product or service. Continuous process improvement encourages all health care team members to continuously question how they and their system are performing and whether performance can improve (Edwards et al., 2008). Data, transparency, and accountability are critical enabling factors for a learning culture, which requires the creation of a structured approach to process and outcome evaluation.

CHALLENGES AND BARRIERS

Even in the face of substantial promise from the application of systems strategies to improve scheduling and access in health care, the committee is fully cognizant of the potential barriers and challenges to achieving the gains possible (see Table 3-1). Many have already been introduced in this report. They include practice and infrastructure barriers, such as those related to the challenge of obtaining reliable data (Kim et al., 2009), the capacity of existing technology (Murray et al., 2003; Pearl, 2014), the lack

TABLE 3-1 Possible Barriers to Implementing Systems Approaches in Health Care

	Practice and Infrastructure Challenges
Data	Metrics for organizational performance and clinical outcomes and systems
Technology	Digital health records designed for data needed, patient portals, telephone consultation systems
	Flexibility to accommodate variable information technology uptake and use by patients
	Staff retraining and rescheduling for telephonic and digital communication with patients
Staffing needs	Need for intervention design teams
	Availability of trained nurses, other non-physician clinicians
	Patient interface personnel, reframing responsibilities, training
Regulatory	Health Insurance Portability and Accountability Act (HIPAA) standards (facility and process redesign standards)
	Cultural Challenges
Preconceptions	Convincing that Lean production works with patient care as well as in manufacturing
Leader buy-in	Belief that systems strategies are evidence-based and refocus existing resources rather than requiring new ones
Staff buy-in	Assurance that retraining and reclassification are not threats and that jobs will not be lost
Patient skills	Need to communicate and educate patients about use of new practice procedures
Organizational	Moving organization from siloed, independent, and fragmented to integrated, aligned consultative, with shared accountability

of systems expertise, and the procurement and training of the necessary clinicians and staff (Coleman et al., 2006; Dhar et al., 2011; Jack et al., 2009), and the pressures of organizational and national regulations (Lee et al., 2015; Pearl, 2014). Cultural barriers include those related to preconceptions on the use of industrial systems engineering in complex patient circumstances (Kim et al., 2006), the need for leaders, staff, and patients to develop new skills, and preexisting tendencies for organizational units to prefer to work autonomously (Cima et al., 2011; IOM, 2015; Kim et al., 2006, 2009; Krier and Thompson, 2014; Lee et al., 2015; Meyer, 2011; Murray et al., 2003). In each, committed leadership is critical to identifying and addressing these issues.

4

Building from Best Practices

EXPERIENCES IN SERVICE EXCELLENCE

There are a number of emerging best practices associated with systems approaches, and the committee believes that testing, disseminating, and applying these best practices to various systems approaches to improving access and wait times is currently the most promising approach to making progress in this aspect of health care. Therefore, in this chapter the committee describes some emerging best practices in systems approaches that can be applied to the health care sector.

Identifying Emerging Best Practices

The committee identified case examples and innovative systems models that have been shown in limited settings to improve scheduling and wait times while having either neutral or positive effects on the quality of care and on the patient experience. With further research, these models have the potential to be adopted more widely and to become a foundation for standards of care. Such examples are found in all specialties, in all care delivery settings, and in different business models and geographic regions. The committee believes the changes illustrated in these examples can usually be achieved without significant additional investments in personnel or facilities, relying instead on process reengineering, resource reallocation, and behavioral change strategies within the individual settings.

Although national standards for access and wait times do not currently exist, the committee did also identify examples of organization-specific

> **BOX 4-1**
> **Representative Benchmarks by Setting**
>
> - **Primary care:** Same- or next-day engagement for new and returning patients, contingent on their needs and preferences.
> - **Primary care backup for urgent services:** Providers who are unable to see patients for urgent services within 48 hours refer them to others.
> - **Specialty care:** Third next available waits of 10 days or less for specialty care new visits. For specialty care visits accompanied by greater sense of patient urgency (e.g., oncology), waits of no more than one day for new patients.
> - **Emergency departments:** Ten-minute door-to-provider time (contact with a provider will occur within 10 minutes of patient arrival at an emergency room).
> - **Hospital admissions from emergency department:** Holding time in the emergency department should not exceed 4 hours after a decision to admit.
> - **Hospital discharge assessment:** Discharge planning begins immediately after admission and initial discharge assessment is completed in the first 24-48 hours of admission.

benchmarks within various health care settings. For example, some organizations set internal benchmarks of same-or next-day engagement for new and returning patients in primary care (Southcentral Foundation's Alaska Native Medical Center) or first time appointments of newly diagnosed cancer patients (Dana-Farber/Brigham and Women's Cancer Center in Boston);[1] internal benchmarks guide door-to-provider times within emergency departments (Virginia Mason Hospital), wait times for specialty new visits (Cincinnati Children's Hospital), and primary care backup practices for urgent services (Tufts Health Plan Network Health). The Joint Commission has also developed standards pertaining to emergency department boarding times and hospital discharge risk assessments. Organization-specific benchmarks, such as these, serve as promising reference points for future research and validation.

Box 4-1 presents these representative benchmarks and is followed by detailed information on various examples of innovative system models that have demonstrated promise in improving health care operations and performance.

---

[1] This information was provided in a Dana-Farber Cancer Institute news release: http://www.dana-farber.org/Newsroom/News-Releases/dana-farber-brigham-and-women%E2%80%99s-cancercenter-now-offers-next-day-appointments-for-new-patients.aspx (accessed June 5, 2015).

Ambulatory Care

The committee has identified best practices for an immediate responsiveness approach to new or returning primary and specialty care patients. These include scheduling strategy models, such as working toward same-day engagement and continuous monitoring and matching capacity and demand, and activities intended to achieve the optimal alignment of supply and demand, including team-based workforce improvement strategies and technology-based alternatives to in-person visits.

Scheduling Strategy Models

Open access/same-day scheduling The advanced access model of patient scheduling, also known as open access or same-day scheduling, has as a core principle that patients can obtain an appointment on the same day if desired (Murray and Berwick, 2003). Appointments are not booked weeks or months in advance, but rather each day starts with a sizable share of the day's appointments being open, with the remainder being appointments for people who elected not to come to the office on the day they called. This workflow model involves only one primary care appointment type. In the early stages of implementation, appointments are divided into two queues or groups of patients, one dedicated to that day's urgent demand and the other open for appointments made when patients called on previous days but did not wish to come in on that day (Murray and Berwick, 2003).

Successful use of the open access model requires accurate forecasting, an engaged team of schedulers and providers, and a carefully determined transition plan. It also requires a commitment, as demonstrated by Baylor Family Medicine (see Box 4-2), to significantly transform scheduling practices. As outlined in Appendix A, the phases of the advanced access method include the initial measurements necessary to determine demand and capacity, the steps for matching demand and capacity, and a transition strategy to scheduling for same-day access, as well as lessons learned on the maintenance of the method and contingency planning.

An effective transition to this model requires the disciplined measurement of demand and capacity, the addition of providers if there is a permanent mismatch of demand and capacity, and the elimination of appointment types. Of key importance in the transition is the elimination of the unnecessary patient backlog, that is, of those patients who have been booked for future visits as a result of an insufficient supply of same-day or next-day visits. Eliminating this backlog requires a temporary increase in patient visits each day until the backlog is eliminated. As the backlog is eliminated, which may require several months, patients are told to call the office when they are ready to be seen, and future appointments cease

> **BOX 4-2**
> **Examples of the Advanced Open Access Model in Primary Care**
>
> **Southcentral Foundation's Alaska Native Medical Center**
> Southcentral Foundation's Alaska Native Medical Center had some patients who waited hours for acute care or months for nonurgent appointments. To decrease wait times, the center's managers took the following steps: matched patients with physicians, actively worked to address the appointment backlog, developed surge contingency plans, encouraged continuity of care, and adjusted the workforce by assigning tasks to non-physicians (Murray et al., 2003). Now that advanced access scheduling has been implemented, patients are guaranteed same-day appointments if they call before 4 p.m. Although it took months to eliminate the appointment backlog, once it was resolved, roughly half of all appointment slots during the next month were held open for same-day appointments. Implementation challenges included poorly functioning telephones that prevented patients from calling for same-day appointments and, because patients can call for same-day appointments until 4 p.m. daily, a high volume of patients late in the day which can strain clinicians. The keys to successful implementation included the involvement of the entire staff, implementing a data system to track patient access, and technical assistance from outside experts with experience implementing advanced access (Murray et al., 2003).
>
> **Baylor Family Medicine**
> At Baylor Family Medicine, an academic primary care practice, TNA (time until the third next available appointment) ranged from 10 to more than 60 days. When planning to implement advanced access, the practice's projection was told that it would take 11 months to work down the backlog. Matching daily supply and demand in the face of the day-to-day variation in physician availability was also a challenge. To address these implementation challenges, Baylor Family Medicine opted to set a "go live" date for advanced access scheduling and, beginning 3 months prior to the "go live" date, made no appointments past that date. To give patients some flexibility in scheduling appointments, the practice also established a 5-day appointment window, which allowed patients to schedule either a same-day appointment or one in the next 5 days. Patients requiring follow-up appointments were told to call to make that appointment when they were ready to be seen, and the practice established a system to send patients reminders for necessary appointments. Patients were given access to their physicians' clinic schedules through the phone system, in a printed handout, and on the practice's website. The practice also established rules for provider leave, established a new process for complete physical exams, and maintained existing staffing levels. Baylor developed a daily activity report to review daily scheduling and monitor appointments over the coming 5 days. The changes reduced the length of the third next available appointment from an average of 17 days to 1 day, which the practice has sustained for more than 2.5 years (Steinbauer et al., 2006).

to exist. Using this model sustainably requires a deliberate and continuous evaluation of supply and demand and a recognition that the model is a quality improvement method that requires dedicated time and personnel within the practice. It also requires a significant change in thinking about how scheduling occurs—to a model where appointments are available in the near term rather than weeks of months into the future. Despite these implementation challenges, a systematic review found that implementing the advanced access model reduces wait times and no-show rates, although patient satisfaction outcomes are mixed (Rose et al., 2011). Box 4-3 describes case studies of how two primary care practices, Southcentral Foundation's Alaska Native Medical Center and Baylor Family Medicine in Houston, Texas, have implemented the advanced access model to improve scheduling and reduce wait times.

The smoothing flow scheduling model A different approach to achieving same-day access uses the operations management technique of smoothing flow. This method identifies and quantifies the many types of variability in patient flow (demand) and identifies the resources available to different

---

BOX 4-3
Example of the Smoothing Scheduling Flow Model in Primary Care

St. Thomas Community Health Center
   St. Thomas Community Health Center, a consortium of safety net practices throughout New Orleans, Louisiana, offers an example of system capacity management in the ambulatory setting. Following the passage of the Affordable Care Act, the amount of uninsured patients at the center increased from 18 percent to greater than 35 percent by early 2014. With fixed financial resources provided by Medicaid and clinic reimbursement rates averaging $30 per visit, the consortium needed ways to be more efficient and cost-effective. At the direction of the chief executive officer, techniques to smooth patient demand were used to improve practice capacity and performance. Improvement efforts based on the science of operations research targeted the widespread variability in the clinics. The methods were focused on improving efficiencies with both appointment setting and patient visits in order to increase throughput and flow. St. Thomas experienced a 35 percent increase in appointment capacity and a 25 percent increase in clinic visits. Increased efficiency has also resulted in reduced patient wait times, additional time slots for same-day and next-day appointments, and improved patient, family, and care team satisfaction. Although the improvement efforts were critical for the center's financial stability, they also proved invaluable in optimizing the center's function as a medical home and increasing its ability to provide high-quality care (Rickard, 2015).

patient groups (supply), with the goal of achieving improvements in wait times. Scheduling practices are tailored to minimize the number of appointment types in order to streamline patient visits (Litvak and Fineberg, 2013).

This approach, which can be applied in both primary and specialty care offices (see Boxes 4-3 and 4-4), involves the study of work flow in the office setting and uses smoothing as a form of dynamic control of the patient and work flow. Phase 1 of the approach focuses on balancing resources for the flow of patients with time-sensitive medical and elective or scheduled appointments. Phase 2 turns attention to the challenge of smoothing elective or scheduled patient flow, such as appointments for yearly physicals, immunizations, or blood pressure checks. Phase 3 addresses artificial variability in demand caused by individual priorities in order to ensure that patients are seen in the right setting, by the right provider, at the right time (IHO, 2015; Litvak and Long, 2000). Box 4-3 describes how St. Thomas Community Health Center, a primary care provider in the New Orleans, Louisiana, area, used the smoothing scheduling flow model to target variability in patient flow within a consortium of primary care safety net practices, and Box 4-4 describes how the Cincinnati Children's Hospital and Medical Center used the smoothing scheduling flow model, focusing on improving existing capacity, to improve and continuously monitor scheduling and wait times in its specialty outpatient clinics.

BOX 4-4
Example of the Smoothing Scheduling Flow Model in Specialty Care

Cincinnati Children's Hospital and Medical Center Outpatient Clinic
 Specialty clinics at Cincinnati Children's Hospital faced increasing demand. To balance this demand with their existing supply and thereby improve access, Cincinnati Children's focused its efforts on improving capacity, namely, provider and resource supply (IOM, 2015). The center first analyzed the supply in its clinics. To improve flow, appointments were reduced to two types (new or return visits), supplemental appointments were temporarily added to reduce backlog, clinic operations were standardized, and the center implemented a clinic cancellation policy (Krier and Thompson, 2014). Following implementation of these changes, the medical center was able to achieve its access target of 10 days or less for the third next available appointment for new visits (Krier and Thompson, 2014). Key to implementing these changes was leadership at all levels and engaging clinical leaders of each division. Although the center has been optimized to perform at peak capacity, continuous monitoring is still required. To that end, Cincinnati Children's Hospital has developed several tools, including a scheduling algorithm and an outpatient supply management tool. The center has also found it important to make financial and productivity data available to providers (IOM, 2015).

Reframing Supply-and-Demand Options

Team-based workforce optimization strategies The adoption of Lean and other techniques of continuous quality improvement could potentially help health care systems to become more team oriented. Team-based approaches to providing health care offer a means to provide health care more efficiently (Grumbach and Bodenheimer, 2004; IOM, 2001a; Leape et al., 2009; Wagner, 2000). These approaches all emphasize such concepts as shared goals, clear roles for team members, mutual trust, and effective communication among different parts of an organization, all in an effort to meet the goal of improving efficiency and eliminating waste (Grumbach and Bodenheimer, 2004). Team-based approaches have the potential to improve quality, productivity, efficiency, and satisfaction among both patients and employees (Montebello, 1994). In addition to increasing overall productivity and efficiency, appropriately and safely delegating certain tasks to nonclinician team members can help increase capacity and thereby improve scheduling and decrease wait times (Brandenburg et al., 2015).

Improving the health care workforce requires data for use in forecasting and managing patient demand in order to avoid an artificial provider-driven component. In practice, however, most forecasts are based on historical averages rather than on the use of newer methodologies based on predictive analytics. Workforce optimization also depends on optimally assigning care tasks to the appropriate members of the care team. For example, wait times for an appointment at the outpatient cardiology clinic at a children's hospital were exceeding 40 days until the program was redesigned to include management by pediatric nurse practitioners. After that, not only did wait times decrease in comparison to clinics run by physicians, but patient satisfaction scores remained high (Evangelista et al., 2012). Another study demonstrated the value of using extended role practitioners, such as physical and occupational therapists, to increase capacity and decrease wait times in an arthritis clinic (Passalent et al., 2013). The increased capacity allowed the clinic to accommodate a rise in patient volumes over the 2-year study period and enabled earlier detection and intervention for patients.

Box 4-5 describes how Group Health in the Northwestern United States implemented team-based care using a patient-centered medical home model (which broadened the role of registered nurses and clinical pharmacists) to improve scheduling in primary care and in chronic care management in particular. Within specialty care, the Thunder Bay Regional Medical Center in Ontario, Canada (profiled in Box 4-6), implemented a shared care clinic that co-locates mental health and primary care services in order to increase coordination across primary and mental health care and to reduce barriers to accessing timely mental health services.

> **BOX 4-5**
> **Example of a Team-Based Approach to Scheduling in Primary Care**
>
> **Group Health**
> Group Health is an integrated delivery system serving more than 600,000 patients in Washington State and Idaho (Hsu et al., 2012). Having successfully implemented a patient-centered medical home (PCMH) pilot program at their Seattle clinic, Group Health decided to undertake a large, systemwide transformation and spread the PCMH model to all 26 of its primary care practices over 18 months (Hsu et al., 2012). Following a Lean management approach, Group Health implemented four system-level changes and four practice-level changes. Central to the practice-level changes was a team-based approach to chronic illness management. Providers were organized into physician-led teams. Key to this approach was the development of goal-driven chronic illness collaborative care plans and evaluations (Hsu et al., 2012). Physicians used a standardized, generic, disease-specific template to develop care plans with patients, and aimed to develop a care plan for each patient with a targeted chronic condition (e.g., diabetes, asthma, hypertension, chronic obstructive pulmonary disease). Physicians could also use care plans to identify patients requiring additional support. These patients received counseling and follow-up from a registered nurse or clinical pharmacist on the patient's care team until their condition improved. An evaluation of the prototype reported that patients used more e-mail, telephone, and specialist visits, but fewer emergency department visits, and patients reported greater satisfaction with the quality of their care (Reid et al., 2010).
>
> An analysis of the PCMH spread throughout Group Health's integrated practice was also conducted. Among all adults impacted by the intervention, there was a 123 percent increase in the use of secure electronic message threads, a 20 percent increase in telephone encounters, no statistically significant changes for hospital admissions, and declines in emergency department visits at 1 and 2 years (13.7 percent and 18.5 percent) following the spread (Reid et al., 2013).[a]
>
> ---
> [a] The text in this box has been modified since the prepublication to include additional information about the analysis of the PCMH spread through Group Health's integrated practice.

Technology-based alternatives to in-person visits In the primary care setting, the care team often works to minimize or eliminate delays for each day's telephone appointment requests and return appointment requests. Some have suggested that many of the needs of the patients requesting appointments—both in primary and specialty care—could be addressed by non-physician providers or by phone, via telemedicine, or via mobile health units; these alternatives would not serve as a replacement for a needed visit but rather as an alternative form of health care (Charles, 2000; IOM, 2000;

> **BOX 4-6**
> **Example of a Team-Based Approach to Scheduling in Mental Health Care**
>
> **Thunder Bay Regional Health Sciences Center Shared Care Clinic**
> Because long wait times for mental health care are associated with higher rates of missed appointments and less usage of mental health services overall, Thunder Bay Regional Health Sciences Center decided to implement a shared care model in one of its clinics to reduce wait times for mental health care in the clinics. Shared care for mental health services involves co-locating mental health services within primary care offices. The mental health and primary care providers also shared a common health record, engaged in consultations, and cared for their patients collaboratively. At the Thunder Bay shared care site two full-time mental health counselors and a part-time psychiatrist were added. Primary care physicians referred patients to the mental health services, where the counselors triaged patients to either counseling or psychiatry services, including cognitive-behavioral, psycho-educational, and supportive counseling. Before the establishment of the shared care clinic, the median wait time for mental health care was 97.6 days. For the 3 years after the shared care clinic was established, the median wait time for shared care was just over 30 days, while the median wait time across nonshared care sites was more than 80 days (Haggarty et al., 2012).

Naylor and Imison, 2010). This approach could be used in particular as a way to deal with issues in rural and underserved areas.

Technology can improve patient access to health care both directly and indirectly (IOM, 2012). Telemedicine, the use of electronic information and technologies to support direct clinical services, can be used as an alternative to an in-person visit to a physician and as a way to improve access at a lower cost (Charles, 2000; IOM, 2000). The development of virtual care platforms has made possible a variety of new care models, including electronic-visits, video chat consultations, and other approaches to home-based care. One key to expanding the use of these models will be the development of new payment models to ensure that providers are properly reimbursed and incentivized to install and use these capabilities in their practices. It will also be necessary to develop a technology infrastructure that makes it possible to track, report on, and provide oversight of these patients and their care.

Patient-tracking technologies can help caregivers work more efficiently and improve patient safety by providing real-time information on a patient's location in the hospital system and identifying obstacles to smooth and timely patient flow (Dobson et al., 2013). Interoperable and interactive health information technology systems can alert a care team of missed appointments to a referring specialist, the presence of new results, or the need for follow-up appointments. Patients can receive reminders of upcoming appointments, manage their prescriptions, or schedule their own appointments (Pearl, 2014).

Technology can assist in the ambulatory environment by routing some office visits to telemedicine visits, with the patients being examined by a virtual clinician; such telemedicine options range from uploading a smart phone photo (e.g., of a skin rash) and sending an e-mail question to the clinician, to sending data from a personal device to the office. One important use of technology will be found in the prework portion of a health care visit. Patients could have a virtual previsit interview to determine the appropriate provider and time for a visit, the need for laboratory or testing in advance of the visit, the need for a medical record screen for outstanding specialist visits and reports, and the transportation needs of patients.

Box 4-7 provides details about how Teladoc in California, Kaiser Permanente Northern California (KPNC), and Virginia Mason Medical Center in Seattle, Washington, have all used technology-based alternatives to improve access to timely primary and specialty care, especially care outside regular business hours. Teladoc, a telemedicine provider with consultant physicians who have no regular relationships with the patients or their regular providers, provides round-the-clock consultations with licensed physicians via telephone or secure Internet video. KPNC offers patients access to providers in primary and secondary care via secure e-mail, telephone, or Web-based video in lieu of and in addition to regular office visits. Virginia Mason Medical Center uses a telephone triage tool to facilitate immediate access to urgent care and to improve scheduling for primary and secondary care appointments for patients presenting with headache symptoms.

Inpatient and Emergency Care Scheduling Strategies

The strategies for implementing an immediate responsiveness approach to inpatient and emergency care patients fall into several categories: admission strategies, care coordination strategies, and the use of predictive models.

Admission Strategies

As described below, some hospitals have redesigned operating room environments to balance resources and the flow of time-sensitive surgical cases with elective scheduled surgeries (Litvak and Fineberg, 2013; Litvak and Long, 2000). The focus of these efforts is to improve access to the operating rooms, emergency department, intensive care unit, and telemetry

> **BOX 4-7**
> **Examples of Technology-Based Alternatives to
> In-Person Primary Care Visits**
>
> **Teladoc**
>   Teladoc is a large telehealth provider in the United States offering 24-hour access to consulting Teladoc physicians via telephone or Internet video. Teladoc physicians have no established relationship with patients, but patients are matched with physicians licensed to practice in their state. To use Teladoc, patients must create an online account and enter their medical history. Patients can then request either a phone or video consultation with a Teladoc physician whenever they need care. Physicians typically respond to requests within 20 to 25 minutes of receiving the request. In April 2012 the California Public Employee's Retirement System began offering Teladoc consultations as a covered benefit with no copayment to members enrolled in its Blue Shield of California health insurance plan. An early evaluation of Teladoc among these users found that less than 1 percent of eligible members used Teladoc in the first 11 months of coverage; similarly, Teladoc visits made up less than 1 percent of total monthly visits to offices, to emergency departments, and via Teladoc combined. The evaluation found that more than one-third of Teladoc visits occurred on weekends or holidays, which was similar to the rate of weekend and hospital emergency department visits (36 percent) and substantially higher than the rate for office visits (8 percent). The top three diagnostic categories were for acute respiratory illness, urinary tract infections and urinary symptoms, and skin problems. This suggests that Teladoc can help increase access to after-hours primary care while also diverting non-urgent care away from emergency departments. Moreover, 21 percent of Teladoc visits were made by patients who had no previous health care use in 2011, suggesting that Teladoc could potentially increase access to care for individuals without a regular physician or who have difficulty accessing primary care. Finally, contrary to expectations, Teladoc visits were significantly less likely to result in a follow-up visit for a similar condition than visits to a physician's office or the emergency department. Although this early evaluation is suggestive of the potential for Teladoc to increase access to primary care, Teladoc users were younger, healthier, lived in more affluent neighborhoods than average, and may have fewer access needs than individuals with the greatest challenges accessing primary care, such as those living in rural or socioeconomically disadvantaged areas (Uscher-Pines and Mehrotra, 2014).
>
> **Kaiser Permanente Northern California**
>   Kaiser Permanente Northern California (KPNC) provides alternatives to in-person office visits via secure e-mail, telephone, or Web-based video. KPNC members can send secure e-mail messages directly to their primary care physicians or to specialist physicians treating them. In addition to asking non-urgent questions in text, patients can attach images and submit completed forms. Frequently, physicians are able to resolve patient's concerns without scheduling inpatient visits. Physicians respond to 83 percent of cases the same day and to 98 percent of cases within 2 business days. For more than a decade, KPNC has
>
> *continued*

BOX 4-7 Continued

offered 10-to-15-minute telephone visits with a physician in lieu of office visits, and patient satisfaction with the telephone visits is high. Finally, encrypted video technology has been adopted by a number of specialty practices. For example, KPNC began offering video visits to provide after-hours care among patients with urgent needs—but not emergency needs—during hours when both regular practices and urgent care clinics are closed. While patients requiring immediate care were directed to go to emergency departments, the physician consulting via video was able to input information from the video consultation in the patient's electronic health record and thereby facilitate the patient's treatment in the emergency department. These alternatives to office visits have the potential to provide high-quality care at a lower cost than in-person care, although the cost savings have yet to be seen. Assessing the effect of these technologies on the quality of care has also been challenging, because they were implemented at the same time as other quality improvement measures. Barriers to implementation include ensuring compliance with the Health Insurance Portability and Accountability Act (HIPAA) standards; differing uptakes by age, race/ethnicity, and region, which makes it necessary to maintain parallel paper, phone, and in-person systems for patients not using virtual technologies; and the need to readjust physicians' schedules to accommodate time to respond to patient e-mails (Pearl, 2014).

Virginia Mason Medical Center in Seattle

At Virginia Mason Medical Center in Seattle, Washington, a health system transformation using Lean methodology has been going on since 2002 (Nelson-Peterson and Leppa, 2007). One piece of this effort involved the redesign of care for patients with uncomplicated headaches. Analysis of internal data showed that roughly 80 percent of patients who contacted Virginia Mason with headache symptoms had uncomplicated headaches. Such headaches do not require magnetic resonance imaging (MRI) or other specialized imaging, emergency care, or a consultation with specialists; nonetheless, 14 percent of these patients underwent an MRI (Blackmore et al., 2011). To reduce avoidable visits to the emergency department and specialists as well as unnecessary imaging, Virginia Mason created and deployed a simple telephone triage tool consisting of questions that a lay telephone operator can ask to determine what initial level of care each caller needs. Patients with symptoms like fever or trauma that require immediate evaluation were directed to the emergency department, while all other patients were given the option of a scheduled appointment with either their regular doctor or a clinician in the headache clinic. Analysis of this staged triage intervention showed that a single visit with telephone follow-up was sufficient for the evaluation and initial treatment of most patients with uncomplicated headache and avoided multiple visits and referrals. Evaluation of the program between January and June 2010 found that same- or next-day appointments with the headache clinic nurse practitioner were available for 95 percent of the patients needing care, and patient satisfaction scores of patients leaving the headache clinic averaged 91 percent (Blackmore et al., 2011).

beds as well as to improve the quality of care and to determine the required hospital resources (e.g., nurses, operating rooms, beds).

Smoothing flow scheduling model The same strategy used to smooth variability in patient demand in primary care settings can also be used to improve patient flow in the admission process through providing a more structured and balanced scheduling of elective patients and surgical cases (Litvak and Fineberg, 2013). By balancing resources and the flow of time-sensitive emergency and urgent cases with elective and scheduled surgical admissions, the competition for beds and delays in surgical cases can be improved. The uneven influx of elective surgical cases—for which the standard practice is to schedule as many are requested by surgeons with admitting privileges—is a major reason why the demand for beds often exceeds capacity in inpatient units (Litvak and Fineberg, 2013). Smoothing elective admissions has been shown to be an effective mechanism for improving capacity in a busy hospital (Litvak and Fineberg, 2013). Appendix C includes an admission improvement plan detailing one way to smooth elective and scheduled patient flow, and Box 4-8 describes how Mayo Clinic, Florida, and Cincinnati Children's Hospital Medical Center used the smoothing scheduling flow model to improve surgical capacity.

BOX 4-8
Examples of Smoothing Patient Flow in Inpatient and Emergency Care

Mayo Clinic, Florida, Operating Room Use
Faced with an increasing demand for surgical services, the Mayo Clinic, Florida, used a variability method to increase capacity without building new operating rooms by improving patient flow into hospital operating rooms. First, the surgical team, working with a design team familiar with variability methodology, defined surgical cases as urgent/emergent (cases that due to clinical need must be performed within 24 hours), work-in, or elective. Due to clinical need urgent/emergent cases had to be performed within 24 hours and were further subdivided into five classifications. Work-in cases were defined as those that needed to be performed within 5 days, but not within 24 hours, and were further classified based on clinical versus administrative needs. All other cases were defined as elective. Next, the hospital collected data for 3 months, during which time no changes were made to operating room scheduling procedures. These data were then used to model various scheduling scenarios and allocate rooms to perform urgent/emergent, work-in, or elective cases. For elective rooms, data were also used to

continued

> **BOX 4-8 Continued**
>
> allocate elective operating room block time across rooms and throughout the week to ensure that elective cases were evenly distributed. All existing policies regarding operating room scheduling and functioning were reviewed and modified to align with the redesigned process. The new scheduling procedure was implemented for the entire surgical practice beginning November 1, 2010. The design team managed the implementation, using dashboards covering daily, weekly, monthly, and quarterly data to monitor the program, and they developed decision trees to facilitate real-time scheduling decision making and to manage conflicts. One year after the reengineered scheduling program had gone into effect, surgical volume had increased by 4 percent, representing nearly 500 additional cases annually. Staff overtime decreased by 27 percent, resulting in more than $100,000 in cost savings. The day-to-day variability in surgery case volume and the number of same-day changes to the elective surgery schedule both decreased substantially as well (Smith et al., 2013).
>
> **Cincinnati Children's Hospital Medical Center**
> As is the case in many hospitals, surgeons at Cincinnati Children's Hospital Medical Center scheduled elective surgeries unevenly throughout the week (Litvak and Bisognano, 2011). The hospital chief executive officer used variability methodology to spread these surgeries out over days in order to smooth the flow of patients through operating rooms (Litvak, 2009). By focusing on capacity management and patient flow through the hospital, hospital management was able to achieve a reduction of 28 percent in weekday operating room wait times for emergency and urgent surgical cases, even with an increase in case volume of 24 percent (Litvak, 2009). Furthermore, weekend operating room waiting time fell by 34 percent, despite a 37 percent increase in volume (Litvak, 2009). Using a "pit crew" approach to bed management, the hospital management used coordinated team efforts to complete critically important tasks in the minimum amount of time while avoiding errors (Reid et al., 2009; Ryckman et al., 2009). It has been estimated that, if each of the 5,700 hospitals in the United States achieved only 10 percent of the financial savings that Cincinnati Children's did through this approach, the U.S. health care system would avoid $57 billion in capital costs associated with building new operating rooms and hospital bed occupancy would increase from 65 percent to greater than 80 percent, enough to provide hospital care for every American lacking health insurance (Litvak and Bisognano, 2011).

Implementing a Coordinated Approach to Care

Care coordination is a strategy to improve effectiveness, efficiency, and quality in health care (Bodenheimer, 2008; Hall et al., 2013; IOM, 2001a). Increased care coordination has the potential to prevent unnecessary delays by eliminating redundancies and inefficiencies (Bodenheimer, 2008). Care coordination is particularly critical at various transitions, such as between providers. In the hospital and post-acute setting, coordinating care is particularly important at discharge. Thus care coordination interventions that have nurses or other non-physicians deliver and coordinate care after discharge, that promote patient self-management in the community, or that otherwise facilitate comprehensive discharge planning can improve patient flow through hospitals by both improving output flow (i.e., assuring timely discharge) and preventing readmissions (Coleman et al., 2004, 2006).

Box 4-9 contains two case studies of organizations that applied a coordinated approach to improving scheduling and wait times in inpatient and emergency care. Specifically, the box describes the UPMC Health System Patient and Family Centered Care Method, which established

---

BOX 4-9
Examples of Coordinated Approach to Improving Scheduling and Wait Times in Inpatient and Emergency Care

UPMC Health System Patient- and Family-Centered Care Method
UPMC Health System, formerly the University of Pittsburgh Medical Center, is a nonprofit, integrated delivery system containing 20 hospitals, outpatient sites, and a health insurance division (Meyer, 2011). Anthony DiGioia, an orthopedic surgeon at UPMC in Pittsburgh, and colleagues developed a care process, the Patient and Family Centered Care Method, to improve patient experiences in the hospital's orthopedic program (DiGioia et al., 2010). The method has six steps: (1) selecting a care experience; (2) establishing a care experience guiding council; (3) evaluating the current state of the care experience using tools such as patient shadowing, care flow mapping, patient storytelling, and patient surveys; (4) developing a working group to develop an improvement strategy; (5) creating a shared vision of the ideal patient and family care experience; and (6) identifying improvement projects and assigning project teams (DiGioia et al., 2010). In 2007, UPMC Presbyterian used the method to improve its trauma service care experience. The staff at UPMC Presbyterian began by establishing a PFCC trauma care guiding council, which identified cervical spine collar clearance as an initial project area. A multidisciplinary working group composed of representatives from a variety of professions including: nursing, parking operations, admissions, pharmacy, corporate communications, and physical therapy was then established for this project (DiGioia et al., 2010). The working group shadowed patients and their families and conducted care flow mapping. Next, they mapped out an ideal care experience from the perspective of patients and families. Based on these activities, the working group created a prioritization process for patients requiring cervical spine collar clearance, upgraded the health information technology system for online X-ray reading, and implemented an alert system that uses pager

continued

BOX 4-9 Continued

messages to notify care managers about potential avoidable delays or avoidable hospital days (for which there were an existing process and existing resources) (DiGioia et al., 2010). Within 2 weeks of appointing the working group, wait times for cervical spine collar clearance for priority patients had been cut in half, from 26.5 to 12 hours. In addition, patient satisfaction rates for the emergency department, general trauma inpatient unit, and trauma step-down unit all increased roughly 10 percent (from 77 to 87.4 percent for the emergency department, 70.3 to 79.7 percent for general trauma, and 68.3 to 72.5 percent for trauma step-down) (DiGioia et al., 2010). There are various implementation challenges, particularly as the hospital system scales up the intervention, and one of the more important is getting buy-in from leadership at all levels—specifically, getting hospital executives and departmental leadership to understand that the method is intended to make better use of existing resources and not to increase costs with new purchases (Meyer, 2011). Despite these challenges, the program has since been applied widely to other departments in eight hospitals in the UPMC Health System.

Boston Medical Center

Boston Medical Center is a large, urban, safety net hospital that wanted to reduce the rates of rehospitalizations and emergency room visits after discharge. To improve discharge services, the hospital implemented a program called re-engineered discharge (RED). The RED intervention is built around nurse discharge advocates and clinical pharmacists. Nurse discharge advocates are trained using a standardized manual with scripts and practice sessions to coordinate the discharge plan within the hospital and to educate patients about and prepare them for discharge. Specific activities include making appointments for post-discharge clinician follow-up or testing, coordinating who will follow up with results from any pending tests, confirming the medication plan, reviewing processes for what to do if problems occur, and ensuring that each discharge plan is aligned with national standards. The nurses then assemble information gathered from these activities into an after-hospital care plan, an illustrated, individualized booklet designed to be accessible to individuals with low health literacy. Following scripts and using teach-back methodology, the nurses review the after-discharge care plan with patients prior to discharge. On the day of discharge, nurses send both the after-hospital care plan and the discharge summary to the patient's primary care provider. Two to 4 days after discharge, a clinical pharmacist calls the patients, making at least three attempts to reach them, and follows a scripted interview with them to review the discharge plan. The pharmacist also reviews medications by asking the patients to bring their medications to the phone, addresses potential problems, and reports any issues to the patient's primary care provider or nurse discharge advocate. Results from a randomized study found that patients participating in the RED intervention were significantly less likely to have a subsequent hospitalization than patients under usual care. Patients participating in RED also reported a higher follow-up rate with their primary care physician (62 percent) compared to usual care patients (44 percent). The intervention also resulted in cost savings of roughly one-third, compared to usual care (Jack et al., 2009).

multidisciplinary teams to identify priority areas, obtain patient and family input, and address wait times for cervical spine collar clearance for priority patients, as well as a program at the Boston Medical Center that used nurses and clinical pharmacists to improve discharge processes.

Use of Systems and Simulation Models

Simulation models use a set of rules, or assumptions, to forecast how different scenarios will play out and can be used as a planning tool to match hospital capacity to patient need (Everett, 2002). In the case of inpatient or emergency department planning or scheduling, these assumptions may cover such things as the number of patients, the interval between patients, the number of staff, the number of operating rooms, and the number of patient beds. Working from these assumptions, simulation models can then examine the effect of various hospital staffing configurations on patient flow (Jones and Evans, 2008). Different scenarios can then be compared in order to identify optimal scheduling scenarios (Kolker, 2008). Simulation models can also be used to model how individual patients move through a health care unit. By showing patient flow, simulation models can help identify bottlenecks and indicate ways to improve patient flow and decrease delays (Coats and Michalis, 2001; Stainsby et al., 2009).

Emergency departments have used a variety of techniques, including Lean (the Toyota Production System) to guide redesign efforts (Holden, 2011). As discussed in Chapter 3, Lean is a method to achieve continuous improvement which identifies the features of a system that create value and those that create waste. Lean processes can be used to identify and continuously monitor inefficiencies that may lead to imbalances in patient demand and hospital capacity that in turn lead to delays in patient flow and thus increased wait times, although additional research is needed about the opportunities and implementation challenges associated with modeling for the purposes of predicting and improving scheduling practices. Box 4-10 describes how Grady Memorial Hospital in Atlanta, Georgia, used systems engineering techniques to re-engineer the hospital's emergency department and how Mayo Clinic, Rochester, used Lean and Six Sigma methods to improve surgical processes.

Scheduling Models in Post-Acute Care

Systems approaches and tools from systems engineering applied to scheduling in primary and acute care can also be applied to post-acute settings such as rehabilitation hospitals and skilled nursing facilities. Increased care coordination, the use of multidisciplinary teams, and alternative approaches to in-person visits are all strategies that can be used to improve

> **BOX 4-10**
> **Examples of Employing Systems Engineering Techniques to Predict and Monitor Work and Patient Flow in Inpatient and Emergency Care**
>
> **Grady Memorial Hospital**
> Grady Memorial Hospital in Atlanta, Georgia, is the fifth-largest safety net hospital in the United States; the hospital serves a population with diverse socioeconomic groups, and before the implementation of the Affordable Care Act only 8 percent of patients whom Grady Hospital served were covered by private insurance. Struggling to remain financially solvent, in 2008 Grady management in collaboration with operations researchers undertook a seven-step process to reengineer emergency department operations. This included process mapping of emergency department patient and work flow; analyses of patient arrival, emergency department service processes, and hospital data; the development of a predictive analytic framework to assess patient admissions demands; the application of a simulation model to improve the emergency department system performance; the identification of system improvements for implementation; and the evaluation of system improvements. The optimization model identified several areas for system improvements, of which the hospital adopted the following: combining registration and triage for certain patient groups, reducing laboratory and X-ray turnaround time, optimizing staffing, eliminating batching of patients to bring from walk-in to one of various treatment zones, and establishing a walk-in center to treat non-urgent patients. These changes resulted in a 33 percent reduction in average length of stay, a 70 percent reduction in average wait time, an increased annual throughput across the emergency department, a 32 percent reduction in the number of patients who left without being seen, a 28 percent decrease in avoidable 72-hour and 30-day readmissions among patients with emergency and urgent conditions (Emergency Severity Index acuity levels 1 through 3), and substantial cost savings. Grady Memorial Hospital has subsequently applied this methodology to other units. The emergency department model has also been implemented in 10 other emergency departments, in which performance and clinical outcomes have been similar to those seen at Grady (Lee et al., 2015).
>
> **Mayo Clinic, Rochester**
> Mayo Clinic, Rochester, is an academic medical center with 88 operating rooms in two acute care hospitals (Cima et al., 2011). To improve operating room efficiency, Mayo Clinic, Rochester, used Lean and Six Sigma methods to implement a surgical process improvement intervention. The hospital first developed a value-stream map of patient flow through operating rooms that detailed event location, personnel, and information technology requirements; alternative pathways; and key performance elements (Cima et al., 2011). A multidisciplinary leadership team then analyzed the map and identified five work streams to organize process improvements:

> **BOX 4-10 Continued**
>
> 1. To reduce unplanned variation in elective surgical cases, details about prescheduled cases (e.g., case time and estimated duration) and planned surgeon absences were made available to all surgeons, and each surgical specialty was required to develop a standardized case description.
> 2. To streamline the preoperative process, the hospital developed standardized preoperative assessment criteria, staggered operating room start times (assigned to each operating room and did not change) and respective report times, and staggered patient entry through three self-triaging check-in lines based on report time.
> 3. To reduce time in operating rooms spent on nonsurgical tasks, the hospital implemented parallel processing, in which these tasks were performed in parallel with ongoing cases in non-operating rooms. The hospital also established targets for turnover time between cases and posted weekly performance metrics outside each operating room monthly.
> 4. To reduce redundancies in patient documentation, the hospital streamlined its electronic health record in which information collected earlier in the preoperative process was automatically put into future records.
> 5. Finally, to ensure staff engagement, the hospital established a communication council composed of representatives from all stakeholders that developed and delivered consistent communication plans to stakeholders and resolved concerns. The hospital also conducted staff satisfaction surveys.
>
> The surgical process improvement intervention resulted in significantly fewer wait times of longer than 10 minutes at surgical admissions, significantly higher rates of on-time arrival to the preoperative area, and significantly quicker operating room turnover times. Furthermore, these efficiency improvements resulted in better financial performance and the need for fewer nursing and other non-clinical staff for daily operations, and late shift and overtime needs among surgery and anesthesia nurses decreased despite an increased surgical volume. Despite efficiency and effectiveness gains, there was a need for enhanced staff support/liaison efforts, with three-fourths of respondents to a staff satisfaction survey reporting that the improvement program increased their efforts and staff expressing concerns about job security even though no nursing or allied health staff were either laid off or reassigned to other work (Cima et al., 2011).

scheduling and patient flow and to decrease wait times. Similarly, as is the case in both primary and acute care settings, systems engineering tools that facilitate system-wide assessments and adjustments can be used to streamline patient flow in post-acute care (Litvak and Fineberg, 2013). For example, the Veterans Affairs Polytrauma Telehealth Network (profiled in Box 4-11) supports increased access and care coordination in post-acute care by using video teleconferencing and peer-to-peer networking across rehabilitation teams and between patients and specialty care providers.

> **BOX 4-11**
> **Example of Innovative and Emerging**
> **Scheduling Models in Post-Acute Care**
>
> **Veterans Affairs Polytrauma Telehealth Network**
> Injuries sustained in combat during Operation Iraqi Freedom and Operation Enduring Freedom are of unprecedented severity and complexity, and they frequently require long-term rehabilitation; some combat-wounded veterans will require rehabilitative services for the rest of their lives (Darkins et al., 2008). The reduction in time between sustaining a battlefield injury and arrival for care in the United States further complicates the rehabilitative needs of combat-wounded veterans. To meet this need, in 2006 the Department of Veterans Affairs (VA) established a telerehabilitation system consisting of four polytrauma rehabilitation center (PRC) hub sites that support 21 regionally based polytrauma network sites (PNSs). The Polytrauma Telehealth Network (PTN) was established to make specialist expertise in PRCs available at PNSs and to coordinate rehabilitation services across sites. PTN is intended to provide comparable or enhanced quality of care at the same or lower cost. Specifically, PTN supports videoconferencing and peer-to-peer networking of rehabilitation teams across the VA, links care across the VA sites and also to Department of Defense counterparts (e.g., Walter Reed Army Medical Center and Bethesda Naval Hospital), allows patients and their families to access distant VA sites (e.g., for specialty care), and supports multicasting for clinical and education activities (e.g., grand rounds). For severely injured patients who may require acute inpatient care in the early stages of their rehabilitation, PTN can facilitate ongoing outpatient care with the same providers in later stages while also allowing the patient to live in his or her local community. For less severely injured patients, PTN allows access to specialty care in their local communities (e.g., direct patient care) and also facilitates care coordination across treatment teams. In 2006 the VA provided 37,234 teleconsultations for patients with mental conditions and supported 25,586 telehealth devices for patients at home who would otherwise have required institutional care (Darkins et al., 2008). Since 2006, the program has been expanded to include 5 PRCs, 23 PNSs, 86 Polytrauma Support Clinic Teams, and 39 Polytrauma Points of Contact located at VA medical centers nationally (VA, 2015b).

Engaging Patients and Families in Systems Design and Implementation

As has been emphasized throughout this report, the committee recognizes that it is important for patients to be core partners in systems redesign. Studies have shown that patients' active management of their own health care is associated with the patients' greater satisfaction with their care and with better health outcomes, quality of life, and economic outcomes (Hibbard and Greene, 2013; IOM, 2013). However, as noted in Chapter 1, providing patient-centered care goes beyond consideration and concern in direct care. It requires a delivery system that supports the provision of care that meets patients' needs—and thus one that integrates patient values, experiences, and preferences into the design and governance of the health care organization. Designing such a system requires engaging patients in organizational design and governance as well as in their direct care (Carman et al., 2013).

With regard to scheduling and access, as described in Chapter 3, a patient-centered health care system understands its inherent capacity, patient demand, and variations in this supply and demand; this leads to a system that performs at its optimal capability, including with minimal delays, but that is also sufficiently flexible to handle temporary fluctuations in either its provider supply or patient demand. Engaging patients in the assessment, design, and improvement processes can lead to a better understanding of patient demand and thus how the system can be realigned to meet that demand.

Simply implementing an advanced scheduling system is not a patient-centered action unless it strengthens the patient–clinician partnership, promotes trust and collaboration, and facilitates the patient's involvement (Davis et al., 2005). To assess patient experiences and patient satisfaction, including with access and scheduling, health care organizations can use and analyze survey data concerning patient experience and satisfaction, such as data from the Consumer Assessment of Healthcare Providers and Systems (CAHPS) surveys that were described in Chapter 1. These data can then be used to identify areas of waste or delays and also to inform access improvement activities such as process redesigns. The implementation of partnerships with patient advisors and the development of patient and family advisory councils have proven to be effective ways to gather this essential information; however, other methods are needed to evaluate the patient's ability to obtain ambulatory and office-based appointments quickly.

Currently, little information exists on the effects of patient involvement in access-related improvement activities on either operational or health care outcomes. However, areas in which patients could be included in efforts to improve access and optimize scheduling may include: defining preferences, exploring alternative access strategies, contributing to the design of pilot improvement efforts, helping to shape communication strategies, and interfacing with governance and leadership. Box 4-12 describes how Seattle Children's Hospital incorporated patient and family needs and preferences when designing its scheduling approach.

Additional opportunities to engage patients in scheduling and access include increasing transparency and communication through publishing wait times data and developing information systems to support communication about scheduling and future care needs. Currently, few data are available to patients regarding wait times, whether for scheduling appointments or

> **BOX 4-12**
> **Example of Patient and Family Engagement
> in Design and Evaluation**
>
> **Seattle Children's Hospital**
> For over a decade, Seattle Children's Hospital has used a Continuous Performance Improvement (CPI) program, a modified version of the Toyota Production System that adapted Lean methods for the health care setting, to improve the quality of the health care that it delivers (Hagan, 2011). A core principle of CPI is focusing primarily on patients. In practice, this means examining each process and determining which steps add value to the patient from the patient's perspective and which do not (Hagan, 2011; Stapleton et al., 2009). The hospital also involves patients and their families in many, but not all, of its improvement efforts, and their direct participation early in the improvement process has reinforced the value of their input (Hagan, 2011; Toussaint and Berry, 2013). For example, when the hospital built its new Bellevue Clinic and Surgery Center, input from patients and their families early in the construction process revealed that it was important for parents to be able to stay with their children in the preoperative area. The space was designed and built accordingly, resulting in more efficient construction (Toussaint and Berry, 2013). However, patients and their families were not always included in quality improvement activities early on. When Seattle Children's redesigned its ambulatory center, it discovered that despite having reduced appointment wait times by 50 percent, patient satisfaction measures were actually falling (Brandenburg et al., 2015). Further inquiry revealed that many families were less interested in same-day access than in the choice to make an appointment on a more convenient day, and Seattle Children's subsequently changed the scheduling algorithm to include an assessment of family needs and preferences (Brandenburg et al., 2015). Thus, despite the use of multidisciplinary teams including members of executive and clinical leadership (e.g., the chief operating officer, the chief medical officer, and department chairs) and representatives of care teams (e.g., physicians, nurses, and residents) (Stapleton et al., 2009) to improve hospital processes driven by a focus on the patient, without direct patient participation in the process the organization was making inaccurate assumptions about patient preferences (Brandenburg et al., 2015). Leadership is now evaluating other organizational assumptions about patient needs and preferences (Brandenburg et al., 2015).

for receiving on-time care at the time of an appointment; similarly, there are few data available concerning which systems are achieving the best results with reducing wait times (Brandenburg et al., 2015). The transparency of such data could potentially help patients make better-informed decisions about their care. Patient-centered care requires communication and education, such as providing patients with details on recommended treatment plans and on the need for and availability of future appointments. The integration of care plans, scheduling, and automatic reminders is a promising application of information technology that could improve access and scheduling throughout the care continuum (Pearl, 2014).

COMMONALITIES IN SUCCESS

This chapter has explored a range of potential approaches and strategies for achieving timely care access across different populations and health care institutions. Because of the nature of the access challenge and the diversity of care settings, it is necessary to employ strategies that can be adapted to local conditions and that are flexible enough to meet changing needs. In the ambulatory care setting, best practices prioritize same-day care and rapid response to ensure that capacity is aligned with demand. Inpatient and emergency care are more variable, so that both care coordination strategies and more sophisticated analyses using predictive modeling may be required. Post-acute care presents an even higher level of variability and may benefit from strategies that prioritize multidisciplinary approaches and developing alternatives to in-person visits that meet patients' needs. Based on a review of the cases as well as the scan of the literature presented in Chapters 2 and 3, the committee identified a number of commonalities among exemplary practices that serve, in effect, as a set of basic health care access principles for primary, specialty, and hospital and post-acute care scheduling (see Box 4-13). These basic access principles are as follows:

Supply–demand matching. A formal and ongoing quantitative assessment of supply and demand is the first principle in providing timely appointments for each request requiring a visit. As described in detail in Chapter 3, measuring and then balancing supply and demand at each step along the care continuum is essential to efficient and effective health care and is also the basic component of a systems approach to managing scheduling and

---

BOX 4-13
Basic Access Principles for All Settings

- **Supply–demand matching** through formal ongoing evaluation.
- **Immediate engagement** and exploration of need at time of inquiry.
- **Patient preference** on timing and nature of care invited at inquiry.
- **Need-tailored care** with reliable, acceptable alternatives to clinician visit.
- **Surge contingencies** in place to ensure timely accommodation of needs.
- **Continuous assessment** of changing circumstances in each care setting.

access to health care. Predictive analyses and simulation models are potentially helpful mathematical tools that health care organizations can use to assess patient demand and to project optimum capacity (see Box 4-8).

Immediate engagement. Every patient or family request for care should be engaged upon inquiry, with a query concerning what the problem is and what might be helpful in the moment. "Immediate engagement" may result in setting a goal of same-day appointments in primary care (see Box 4-2), in specialty care clinics meeting their internal scheduling goals of 10 days or less (see Box 4-4), or in practices that seek alternatives to in-person visits to meet immediate, non-emergent needs (see Box 4-5).

Patient preference. Patients should be invited to express their preferences on the timing of the care interaction (Berry et al., 2014). As detailed in Chapter 3, the focus on meeting patient need should drive systems strategies aimed at improving health care, and systems-based approaches to improving health care scheduling and access should be aimed to improve the patient experience and meeting patients' needs, as defined by patients themselves. At UPMC Health System (see Box 4-9), the collection and analysis of patient preference data, assembled using such methods as patient shadowing, patient storytelling, and patient surveys, is an important component of the institutional strategy to improve access. As was the case with Seattle Children's Hospital (see Box 4-12), patient preference data contributed to the redesign of the health system's existing systems program.

Need-tailored care. The options for same-day response should include various proven methods for meeting patients' needs or concerns. As described in Chapter 3 and presented in the examples above, these tailored methods for providing immediate engagement may incorporate evolving technologies in health care for the scheduling and delivery of care, including providing various options for in-person visits with physicians such as phone calls, e-mails, teleconferences, telehealth, e-prescribing, and other forms of e-consults (see Box 4-7). Other methods may use non-physician clinicians such as nurses and clinical pharmacists in new capacities (see Boxes 4-5 and 4-9).

Surge contingencies. Every practice setting should have contingency provisions for accommodating patients' acute clinical problems or questions that cannot be addressed in a timely manner. As discussed in the examples above, technology-based alternatives to in-person visits (e.g., phone calls and videoconferences) to treat urgent but not emergency medical issues after regular office hours have been shown not only to meet patients' immediate concerns but also to allow consultant physicians to ensure the continuity of care by, for instance, scheduling follow-up in patient visits with the patient's regular doctor and entering clinical notes and messages for the patient's regular doctor through an interoperable electronic health record (see Box 4-7).

Continuous assessment. Patient access metrics—including data on patient and family experience and satisfaction, scheduling practices, patterns, and wait times, cycle times, provision and performance experience for alternative care models, and effective care continuity—should be collected, evaluated, and reported for each practice and clinic. The data collected within each health care organization can serve as tools for evaluating daily activity and monitoring appointments over a specified time period (see Box 4-2), or data can be used to design and test various scheduling models (see Box 4-8). Moreover, to facilitate the interoperability and assessment of comparative performance across care settings, standards and benchmarks on access and wait times should also be developed, tested, and implemented with the assistance of national organizations with expertise in standards development and testing.

CAPACITY IMPLICATIONS

Standards and Quality Improvement Organizations

Throughout the report, the committee has noted that few standards and measures exist to adequately reflect performance on health care access. Reviewing the current evidence and the current state of health care systems, the committee determined that it is not currently possible to develop a nationwide standard, but instead standards must be tailored to reflect the influences of the specific setting. As the evidence base grows, standards and quality improvement organizations should design more specific measures and standards to complement and even replace the current best practices. It is important that these measures and standards be evidenced-based and achievable.

Under the auspices of the Department of Health and Human Services (HHS), both the Centers for Medicare & Medicaid Services (CMS), and the Agency for Healthcare Research and Quality (AHRQ) provide federal oversight of health care quality throughout the nation and provide the leadership needed to incorporate access and methods for improvement into the national strategy for health care redesign. Together the two agencies can assist with the incorporation of access and the integration of systems strategies and operations management.

A particularly important possibility is that CMS could incorporate access and scheduling elements into its current portfolio of funded projects, including the Center for Medicare & Medicaid Innovation, the Hospital

Inpatient Quality Reporting Program, the Hospital Outpatient Quality Reporting Program, the Physician Quality Reporting System, and other long-term care and ambulatory care projects. AHRQ can further the development of access and performance-based measures and incorporate them into the National Quality Measures Clearinghouse.

Representing the private sector, the National Quality Forum (NQF), the National Committee for Quality Assurance (NCQA), and The Joint Commission offer natural complements to the efforts of the federal agencies to spur attention and needed improvements in health care access. Further improvements can be achieved through the integration of routine measures and standards of access as a starting point of a national health care redesign. As the clearinghouse of performance measurement, preferred practice, and frameworks for health care improvement, NQF is an essential stakeholder in the efforts to implement, assess, and improve the recommendations of this report. Of particular importance will be the role of NQF in the development of access measures, specifically patient experience measures that are linked to outcome. In addition, the integration of systems engineering, capacity management, and operations research into their education and outreach programs will be key to ensuring further development of the field.

As a consensus builder in the field of quality improvement and standards, NCQA can assist in the spread of the best practices described in this report. In particular, NCQA's work with technology development and uptake and with the integration of access measures into the Healthcare Effectiveness Data and Information Set and Consumer Assessment of Healthcare Providers and Systems is essential to the redesign to a patient-centered model of health care. The Joint Commission initiative Outcomes Research Yields Excellence is well suited to integrating access-related performance measures into accreditation for hospitals and retail health care clinics. In addition, the inclusion of access measures into the National Patient Safety Goals, and partnership with patient safety organizations that advocate for transparency for patients and consumers (such as the Leapfrog Group) will be a key to introducing and enforcing national attention to this critical component of health care redesign. See Box 4-14 for additional information on these organizations.

Engaging Stakeholders in Design and Implementation

To successfully apply emerging best practices, health care delivery organizations need the expertise and vision of a range of stakeholders, including patients and families, health care organizations, professional societies, insurers and other payers, and the government. The section below describes key stakeholders that are important for implementing, regulating, and sustaining scheduling approaches.

> **BOX 4-14**
> **Standards and Quality Improvement Organizations**
>
> A variety of organizations are involved in establishing and maintaining standards in health care as well as developing measures for the monitoring and assessment of these standards. Brief descriptions of key standard organizations are provided below.
>
> - The Centers for Medicare & Medicaid Services (CMS) plays an important role in the development of standards through the administration of Medicare, Medicaid, the Children's Health Insurance Program, and related insurance and care programs. This includes standards for providers and organizations nationwide as well as a range of programs aimed at improving quality, safety, and payment in the health system, many of which are housed in the CMS Innovation Center (CMS, 2015a).
> - The Joint Commission is an independent accreditation and certification program for health care organizations. This includes the development and maintenance of standards for health care quality and performance as well as measures to enable evaluation. The Joint Commission conducts on-site surveys of all certified organizations every 2 to 3 years (JC, 2015).
> - The National Committee for Quality Assurance is a care quality organization that administers a variety of programs to support measurement, improvement, transparency, payment reform, and accountability. This includes the accreditation of health plans and the development of measures, standards, and tools for tracking progress and comparing performance, including the Healthcare Effectiveness Data and Information Set (NCQA, 2015).
> - The National Quality Forum is a membership-based organization that endorses health care quality measures. Activities include convening multistakeholder working groups to evaluate measures, seeking continuous feedback on measure performance, and serving as a forum for stakeholders in the health care measurement community (NQF, 2015).

Patients and Families

A key foundation of this report is that patients and their families are essential to the redesign of health care to improve access. Therefore, their preferences should be actively sought and considered when developing and implementing systems approaches to scheduling. Patients and their families can contribute expertise to help clarify patient demand challenges and help seek innovative solutions. Through a number of informal or formal channels (e.g., patient and family advisory councils, surveys, and focus groups), patients and their families can help define preferences, explore alternative access strategies, and contribute to the design of pilot improvement efforts, shape communication strategies, and interface with governance and leadership.

Engineering and Operations Research Leaders

As health care further changes with increased financial uncertainty, a continuing need for improved efficiency, and continued vigilance for high quality and safety, the leaders of systems engineering and operations management could contribute to the redesign of scheduling practices. The role of systems engineering leaders could involve offering education to physician executives and administrative leaders as well as the development of an infrastructure of talent and expertise (Valdez et al., 2010).

Professional Societies

Developing partnerships between providers and systems engineers will require the introduction of professional societies to systems approaches and to their potential applications in health care. Professional societies have enormous potential to drive policy, determine priorities for their members, and provide an important lever of change for leaders within organizations and practices. Participating in joint workshops and education efforts will begin the process of creating an interdisciplinary partnership and developing the field of systems engineering in health care. Research has always been a high priority for professional organizations and could be focused on designing and overseeing a systems engineering portfolio of projects. Professional societies could then assist their members in the development of appropriate projects and the implementation of new methods within their practices and organizations (Valdez et al., 2010).

Insurers and Other Payers

Governmental agencies, including HHS, the Department of Veterans Affairs (VA) and the Veterans Health Administration (VHA), and the Department of Defense's Military Health System together influence the delivery of health care to millions of people in the United States and are intimately involved in a variety of efforts that affect health care access. Together with private insurers, they can play a crucial role in the redesign of health care to improve access and decrease cost (DoD, 2014; Levinson, 2014; Murrin, 2014; Nelson et al., 2014).

Insurance company policies have a significant influence over the delivery of health care. Incentivizing providers and administrators to use the techniques of systems engineering to reduce wasteful processes and to streamline health care would lead to a beneficial partnership for all (Valdez et al.,

2010). Insurers are increasingly partnering with providers in accountable care efforts, and the associated financial support could serve to drive a large number of much-needed improvement activities. Insurers play an essential role in health care access reform because of their interest in having a strong financial performance over a longer period of time. As many of the financial effects resulting from systems engineering approaches accrue over several years with no rapid return on investment, this partnership will require a careful calibration of expectations (Gong et al., 2015).

Government

HHS has provided the impetus for the adoption of health information technology (health IT) through the Health Information Technology for Economic and Clinical Health Act (HHS, 2015). As part of the meaningful use of IT, interoperability has been singled out as an area requiring further development, and it is a factor that will have a direct impact on health care access (McGowan et al., 2012). HHS's role in driving additional changes in IT infrastructure and governmental oversight cannot be overstated. The introduction of additional IT functionality through the Office of the National Coordinator for Health Information Technology to ensure standardized measurement and scheduling would allow successful access reform (ONC, 2015). As the national agency responsible for the training, design, and monitoring of the health care workforce, the Health Resources and Services Administration (HRSA) will play an important role in implementing the recommendations, partnering with professional organizations to educate the health care workforce and offer new roles for members of the care team (HRSA, 2015).

Also under HHS, the CMS Innovation Center is involved in funding many start-up projects investigating new payment and delivery models that align with the triple aim to achieve better care for patients, better health for our communities, and lower costs (CMS, 2015c). CMS has already provided funding for the first group of improvement efforts, including the use of e-Consult and e-Referral, and it will be a valuable partner in overseeing the implementation of the recommendations in the heterogeneous setting of health care (CMS, 2015e). The CMS Partnership for Patients was an important partner for emphasizing the need for the patient-centered focus in care redesign, and it laid an important foundation for how this principle of patient-centeredness can be applied to solving access challenges. Because access reform involves a movement toward patient-centered care, CMS wields strong influence in this movement through funding efforts, spreading success, and generally broadcasting the success of using systems engineering and operations management techniques to address the profound delays within the health care system (CMS, 2015b).

National health care providers are also important for facilitating scale and spread of best practices and expanding the evidence base. As presented in this report, the Department of Defense Military Health System is already studying variability of wait times within its own organization, seeking strategies for geographic barriers, and developing benchmarks for wait times and access (DoD, 2014). The VA/VHA efforts will require significant attention to the roles of leadership and the command and control management found within the organization. However, with some of the new efforts recently put into place and the staged introduction of techniques that were previously successful in various VA/VHA facilities, systems approaches could yield very rich results. In a system combining both financial and clinical data, the VA/VHA is set to be the national leader of integrating systems engineering into health care (VA, 2014a).

The cases presented within this chapter, as well as the literature reviewed by the committee, provide a foundation for the committee's recommendations (presented in Chapter 5), which emphasize the needs to anchor scheduling practices within the identified access principles; to adopt systematic approaches to health care scheduling; to address variation of scheduling practices through coordinated efforts to build the evidence base, test best practices, and develop standards; and to incorporate the perspectives of patients and other stakeholder groups in planning, implementing, and evaluating new approaches to scheduling.

5

Getting to Now

CAPTURING THE MOMENT

As chronicled in the committee's assessment, access and wait time challenges exist for patients and families—as well as for providers—throughout the nation. On the other hand, the committee has found ample potential for positive and far-reaching improvements. The term "Getting to Now" reflects the committee's determination—based on their expertise, models found within other sectors, and the literature and case examples found within health care—that there is currently an opportunity to develop systems-based approaches to scheduling and access that provide immediate engagement of a patient's concern at the point of initial contact. These approaches include use of in-person appointments as well as alternatives like team-based care, electronic or telephone consultations, telehealth, and surge capacity agreements with other caregivers and facilities. To reach the goal of immediate engagement, given the complexity of the health care system and the interdependence of participants and processes, no single stakeholder alone can bring about the changes needed to improve access.

In the face of both the increasing complexity of diseases and interventions and the need for greater efficiency and effectiveness, the roles of health care providers have been changing rapidly, from the traditional model of autonomous practice to the current ideal of collaborative, team-based care. This is a significant change and requires the development of an entirely new mental model, particularly for physicians, who may have little experience or training in team-based care. The application of a systems perspective is a similarly novel concept for practice cultures that have been substantially bounded by their own siloed cultures.

The committee has found that the problems resulting from access and wait time issues go beyond the costs imposed on patients by prolonged wait times, delays in the provision of care, and geographic limitations. These access challenges also generate significant costs associated with the poor quality and waste caused by delays and decreased access. Despite the extent of the challenges, this is an issue that has received little attention, is not routinely measured and reported, and is under-studied. Existing standards for appropriate wait times to get an appointment are few, are based on little evidence, and amount essentially to little more than general reference points.

Still, experiences in various places indicate that the potential exists for progress through process, service, and workforce redesign that need not be resource intensive. Although areas of excellence are steadily becoming more common—including many such areas found in the Department of Veterans Affairs (VA) and the Veterans Health Administration (VHA)—best practices are not yet broadly disseminated, and there has been limited uptake of proven tools and techniques. The collective use of systems strategies, new management approaches, and improved involvement of patients and families can move the current system forward to one that is more patient-centered and can help to provide convenient, efficient, and excellent health care in a variety of settings, without the need for costly investment. As part of the redesign process, decision makers must make creative use of the full range of factors that help to smooth demand and improve supply, including digital technologies, social media, telemedicine, and other new avenues of care delivery. Continuous personal, organizational, and national learning should be the driving forces for improved access, simplified scheduling, and decreased wait times for the nation.

The issues considered by the committee are emblematic of broader challenges and opportunities in health care: e.g., the need to orient all processes and decisions to the perspectives of patients, the importance of taking a systems perspective in dealing with the interplay of complex processes, and the requirements of executive-level leadership to affect change. Each of these challenges is important within the access and scheduling domain. Because change will require broad leadership from stakeholders throughout the nation, the findings and recommendations that follow are targeted to national and health care delivery leaders. With this report, the committee seeks to present both a vision and a roadmap for national progress in this vital area.

COMMITTEE FINDINGS

Throughout this report are various findings related to systemic problems the committee has observed, promising practices it has identified, basic premises for implementation, and the foundations and capacities required for progress (see Box 5-1). The committee's specific findings are presented below.

Variation in Timeliness of Care

Finding: Timeliness in providing access to health care varies widely. Variation ranges from same day in some circumstances to several months in others. This is the product of generally unstructured and nonsystematic

---

BOX 5-1
Summary of Committee Findings

- **Variability:** Timeliness in providing access to health care varies widely.
- **Consequences:** Delays in access to health care have multiple consequences, including negative effects on health outcomes, patient satisfaction with care, health care utilization, and organizational reputation.
- **Contributors:** Delays in access to health care have multiple causes, including mismatched supply and demand, a provider-focused approach to scheduling, outmoded workforce and care supply models, priority-based queues, care complexity, reimbursement complexity, financial barriers, and geographic barriers.
- **Systems strategies:** Although not common practice, immediate engagement for patients is achievable through queue streamlining and related systems strategies to access and scheduling.
- **Supply and demand:** Continuous assessment, monitoring, and realigning of supply and demand are basic requirements for improving health care access.
- **Reframing:** Alternatives to in-office physician visits, including the use of non-physician clinicians and technology-mediated consultations, can often meet patient needs.
- **Standards:** Standardized measures and benchmarks for timely access to health care are needed for reliable assessment and improvement of health care scheduling.
- **Evidence:** Available evidence is very limited on which to provide setting-specific guidance on care timeliness.
- **Best practices:** Emerging best practices have improved health care access and scheduling in various locations and serve as promising bases for research, validation, and implementation.
- **Leadership:** Leadership at every level of the health care delivery system is essential to steward and sustain cultural and operational changes needed to reduce wait times.

approaches to the design, implementation, and assessment of scheduling protocols.

Consequences of Delays in Access to Care

Finding: Delays in access to health care have multiple consequences, including negative effects on health outcomes, patient satisfaction with care, health care utilization, and organizational reputation. These consequences are experienced throughout the U.S. health care system, impact how care is delivered and experienced by patients, and could be substantially diminished.

Causes of Delays in Access to Care

Finding: Delays in access to health care have multiple causes, including mismatched supply and demand, the current provider-focused approach to scheduling, outmoded workforce and care supply models, priority-based queues, care complexity, reimbursement complexity, financial barriers, and geographic barriers.

Systems Strategies

Finding: Although not common practice, immediate engagement for patients is achievable through queue streamlining and related systems strategies to access and scheduling. Contrary to the notion that same-day service is not achievable in most sites, same-day options have been successfully employed through a variety of strategies, when devoted to supply and demand assessments, working through backlogs, and achieving balance in the resource allocations and flow patterns.

Supply and Demand Assessment

Finding: Continuous assessment, monitoring, and realigning of supply and demand are basic requirements for improving health care access. Full accounting of capacity elements, scrupulously monitoring the volume and nature of demand, process redesign aimed at improving patient flow and clinic workflow, and better matching patient needs with available staff skills and duties can improve patient volume and access, decrease the cost of care, and lessen the need to add personnel.

Reframing and Expanding Alternate Supply Options

Finding: Alternatives to in-office physician visits, including the use of non-physician clinicians and technology-mediated consultations, can often meet patient needs. Reframing the supply and demand options is possible also through electronic consultations, telehealth, and surge capacity agreements with other caregivers and facilities.

Lack of Standards for Timely Access to Care

Finding: Standardized measures and benchmarks for timely access to health care are needed for reliable assessment and improvement of health care scheduling. Standards are needed to provide reliable information on comparative performance across various care settings, practices, and circumstances with respect to patient and family experience, including care match with patient goals; scheduling practices, patterns, and wait times; cycle times; the provision of and performance experience regarding alternative care models; and effective care continuity.

Inadequate Evidence

Finding: Available evidence is very limited on which to provide setting-specific guidance on care timeliness. Reliable performance standards cannot be established without better data. To develop the evidence base, health care organizations will need reliable information, tools, and assistance from various national organizations with the requisite expertise—as well as inter-organization coordination to ensure the harmony of reporting instruments and reference resources.

Best Practices for Timely Access to Care

Finding: Emerging best practices have improved health care access and scheduling in various locations and could serve as promising bases for research, validation, and implementation. Although there is not enough available evidence to establish specific standards for scheduling and wait times, innovative systems models and case studies can be identified on the basis of empirical observations of successful practices. With further research into their efficacy, these models have the potential to be adopted more widely and to become the foundation for standards of care.

Leadership

Finding: Leadership at every level of the health care delivery system is essential to steward and sustain cultural and operational changes needed to reduce wait times. Leadership must be devoted to reflecting, sustaining, and enhancing patient-centered care in scheduling and access and the results must be continually gathered, assessed, made available, and deployed in order to drive and reward improvement.

COMMITTEE RECOMMENDATIONS

Based on these findings, the committee offers 10 recommendations that it believes will accelerate progress toward the spirit and the practice of the immediate responsiveness envisioned as health care's goal (see Box 5-2). The committee recommendations are aimed at the widespread adoption of the basic access principles described in Chapter 4 and summarized in Box 5-3: supply matched to projected demand, immediate engagement, patient preference, care tailored to need, surge contingencies, and continuous assessment.

BOX 5-2
Summary of Committee Recommendations

For National Leadership leading to:
1. **Basic access principles** spread and implemented.
2. **Federal implementation initiatives** with multiple department collaboration.
3. **Systems strategies** broadly promoted in health care.
4. **Standards development** proposed, tested, and applied.
5. **Professional societies** leading application of systems approaches.
6. **Public and private payers** providing financial incentives and other tools.

For Health Care Facility Leadership leading to:
7. **Front-line scheduling** practices anchored in the basic access principles.
8. **Governance commitment** to leadership on basic access principles.
9. **Patient and family participation** in designing and leading change.
10. **Continuous assessment** and adjustment at every care site.

BOX 5-3
Basic Access Principles for All Settings

- **Supply–demand matching** through formal ongoing evaluation.
- **Immediate engagement** and exploration of need at time of inquiry.
- **Patient preference** on timing and nature of care invited at inquiry.
- **Need-tailored care** with reliable, acceptable alternatives to clinician visit.
- **Surge contingencies** in place to ensure timely accommodation of needs.
- **Continuous assessment** of changing circumstances in each care setting.

The recommendations that follow are aimed at building the essential foundational elements for the implementation of these basic access principles at the national level and on through to the levels of the individual health care facility. The embedded centerpiece of the recommendations is a focus on the needs of the patient and family, and the development of the skills and tools necessary to lead an organizational culture of service excellence in the execution of that focus.

Recommendations for National Leadership

The committee recommends that

1. National initiatives to address scheduling and access issues related to primary, specialty, hospital, and post-acute care appointments should be anchored in spreading and implementing basic access principles, including: supply matched to projected demand, immediate engagement, patient preference, care tailored to need, surge contingencies, and continuous assessment.

2. With active support and leadership led by the Secretaries of the Department of Health and Human Services, the Department of Veterans Affairs, and the Department of Defense, coordinated federal initiatives should be initiated to draw upon the leadership and resources of the multiple federal agencies that are important to the practical and reliable realization of access principles throughout the nation. These efforts more specifically include

    a. The Secretary of Health and Human Services, in close collaboration with the Secretaries of Defense and Veterans Affairs, should develop and test strategies to move from the office visit as the default site of care delivery to a broader care system, with expanded roles for telehealth, in-home visits, and group visits.
    b. The Agency for Healthcare Research and Quality should strengthen its efforts to identify and disseminate the experiences of organizations with effective, innovative activities to expedite patient access.
    c. The Office of the National Coordinator for Health Information Technology (ONC) should develop and test models of information technology to support the monitoring and analysis of operational data, including access metrics on scheduling and wait times. These data should integrate seamlessly into existing systems and be interoperable to enable communication and data

exchange with other health care organizations and the assessment of comparative performance. ONC should also develop and test analytic tools that can continuously monitor current operational conditions, including the scheduling measures of supply and demand. ONC should provide technical assistance to health care organizations regarding the implementation of these operational data systems and analytic tools.

d. Major federally operated direct clinical service providers, including the Department of Defense and the Department of Veterans Affairs, should work individually and cooperatively to develop and test emerging best practices across different settings and geographic locations. The principles of the most successful models should be widely implemented.

e. The Health Resources and Services Administration should strengthen the capacity of its network of community health centers to share information about successes and failures in efforts to transform access to care, and it should assist with the implementation of the recommendations by partnering with professional organizations to offer education of the health care workforce.

3. All coordinated efforts across federal agencies should include representation from leaders of health care delivery systems, patients and families, and industrial engineering who should work collaboratively with leadership of the federal departments to improve the broad application, assessment, and promotion of systems strategies for continuous learning and improvement in health and health care.

4. Measure developers and accreditors such as the National Quality Forum, the National Committee for Quality Assurance, The Joint Commission, and the Leapfrog Group should collaborate in research and development initiatives to build understanding and action for proposing, testing, and applying standards related to the access principles. These initiatives should include

   a. Capacity assessments (supply)—Assessment should be conducted on staffing levels, exam room capacity, and hours and days of operation.
   b. Patient factor assessments (demand)—Research should be conducted on the various implications of patient numbers, patient query volume, patient timing preferences, and impacts of no-shows.

c. Pilot demonstrations—Alternative approaches should be tested through pilot demonstrations.
d. Systems tools and expertise—Assessment instruments should be developed for use by organizations in identifying and applying systems-oriented practices and professionals.
e. Best practice assessment—Inventories should be developed and assessed on best practices under different circumstances.

5. Professional societies should work with standards and certification organizations to advance professional awareness, understanding, and application of systems approaches, tools, and incentives for the implementation/uptake of systems strategies to assess and improve health care scheduling and access that are grounded in the six access principles. This includes

   a. Engineering partnership models—Models should be developed for partnering with systems engineering professionals for care improvement.
   b. Systems curricular components—Curriculum initiatives should develop modules for incorporating systems approaches into the education of health professionals.
   c. Care access research and demonstration—A research agenda should be developed for demonstration projects to improve insights on the necessary education, skill sets, and cultures that are most conducive to advancing systems approaches to care access.

6. Public and private payers—and employers who pay for care—should be active participants in system improvement through initiatives that encourage creativity and innovation in the implementation and achievement of the access principles. These initiatives include

   a. Payment that is consistent with or supportive of innovative approaches—Payment strategies should be developed to enable innovative access improvement approaches, such as the use of teams, virtual consults, and expanded hours.
   b. Access assurance networks—Support strategies should be developed to encourage access assurance networks, such as interorganization backup and redundancy plans.
   c. Access learning networks—Approaches should be developed to ensure more rapid information sharing concerning successful strategies for access improvement.

Recommendations for Health Care Delivery Systems Leadership

The committee recommends that

7. The front-line scheduling practices of primary, specialty, hospital, and post-acute care appointments should be anchored in basic access principles, including supply matched to projected demand, immediate engagement, patient preference, care tailored to need, surge contingencies, and continuous assessment.

8. The leadership and governing bodies at each level of the health care delivery sites should demonstrate commitment to implementing the basic access principles through visible and sustained direction, workflow and workforce adjustment, the continuous monitoring and reframing of supply and demand, the effective use of technology throughout care delivery, and the conduct of pilot improvement efforts.

9. Decisions involving designing and leading access assessment and reform should be informed by the participation of patients and their families. The potential ways that patients could provide their expertise through informal or formal channels (e.g., patient and family advisory councils, surveys, and focus groups) include contributing input on their expectations, experiences, and preferences for scheduling practices and wait times; helping representatives of health systems explore alternative access strategies; contributing to the design of pilot improvement efforts; helping to shape communication strategies; and interfacing with governance and leadership.

10. Care delivery sites should continuously assess and adjust the match between the demand for services and the organizational tools, personnel, and overall capacity available to meet the demand, including the use of alternate supply options such as alternate clinicians, telemedicine consults, patient portals, and Web-based information services and protocols.

ACCELERATING PROGRESS

Focus on Patient and Family

Achieving meaningful improvement in scheduling and access will depend directly on how engaged patients are in the improvement process. Understanding the demand side of the scheduling equation requires a thorough evaluation of patients' needs and expectations for their care as well as a continuous monitoring of patients' ability to access the care they need. No matter whether one approaches the area from the perspective of the philosophy of the care process, the effectiveness of the clinical outcome, the satisfaction of both patients and clinicians, or the development of patient-controlled health care tools, it is clear that, to an ever-increasing degree, patients have a critical and very active role to play in health care. This role is not limited to their own care but extends to participation in shaping the progress of the nation's health system toward improved quality, efficiency, and access at every stage. Harnessing the engagement and the potential of patient and family leadership for improvements in scheduling and access can be a critical step down the path of the broader culture change that will lead to health care that is more effective and more efficient.

Systems-Oriented Strategies

The committee's exploration of successful case studies and strategies for success revealed a strong potential—and need—for learning from the practices of other sectors in which operations research and systems strategies have transformed overall performance. There is certainly much to be gained through the use of systems strategies in reducing wait times and ensuring adequate and timely access to care while improving the effectiveness and the efficiency of the health care organization. Tools such as Lean and the lessons learned from such industries as aviation and customer service have demonstrated the significant potential that exists in the health care system for gains in efficiency and access. The success in some places of applying queuing theory and engineering models to deal with the complexity inherent in health care scheduling—the diversity of populations served, the range of services provided, and the frequency of no-shows and other anomalies—offers but one example of the importance of a system-wide perspective across all aspects of health care in embedding engineering practices, tools, and skills as a fundamental component of health care that continuously learns and improves.

Leadership

Ultimately, the successful implementation of the committee's recommendations—and of broader efforts to transform performance in health care—will depend on leadership. This certainly means leadership from the top of the organization, at the level of the chief executive officer and board of directors, but it also means leadership involvement from stakeholders in every aspect of health care. Achieving meaningful access will require not only strategic vision at the outset but also sustained attention, assessment, feedback, and initiative at every level of the organization. The basics of a culture of service excellence, with the full involvement of patients and families, commitment to continuous monitoring and assessment, transparency, accountability, and empowering organizational leadership and decision making from participants at every level, will help ensure that every patient—whether they are seeking help immediately or at a later point—receives the right care at the time they need and expect it.

References

AAMC (Association of American Medical Colleges). 2014. *GME funding: How to fix the doctor shortage.* https://www.aamc.org/advocacy/campaigns_and_coalitions/fixdocshortage (accessed December 15, 2014).

Abdel-Aal, R. E., and A. M. Mangoud. 1998. Modeling and forecasting monthly patient volume at a primary health care clinic using univariate time-series analysis. *Computer Methods and Programs in Biomedicine* 56(3):235-247.

ACEP (American College of Emergency Physicians). 2008. *Emergency department crowding: High-impact solutions.* Irving, TX: American College of Emergency Physicians.

Adler-Milstein, J., C. M. DesRoches, and A. K. Jha. 2011. Health information exchange among US hospitals. *American Journal of Managed Care* 17(11):761-768.

Agwunobi, J., and P. A. London. 2009. Removing costs from the health care supply chain: Lessons from mass retail. *Health Affairs* 28(5):1336-1342.

AHRQ (Agency for Healthcare Research and Quality). 2015. *Comparative data: Clinician & group.* https://cahpsdatabase.ahrq.gov/CAHPSIDB/Public/CG/CG_About.aspx (accessed May 20, 2015).

Anhang Price, R., M. N. Elliott, A. M. Zaslavsky, R. D. Hays, W. G. Lehrman, L. Rybowski, S. Edgman-Levitan, and P. D. Cleary. 2014. Examining the role of patient experience surveys in measuring health care quality. *Medical Care Research and Review* 71(5):522-554.

Anupindi, R., S. Chopra, S. Deshmukh, J. A. V. Miegham, and E. Zemel. 2005. *Managing business process flows: Principles of operations management.* Englewood Cliffs, NJ: Prentice Hall.

Armstrong, N., G. Herbert, E. L. Aveling, M. Dixon-Woods, and G. Martin. 2013. Optimizing patient involvement in quality improvement. *Health Expectations* 16(3):E36-E47.

Bell, E. J., S. S. Takhar, J. R. Beloff, J. D. Schuur, and A. B. Landman. 2013. Information technology improves emergency department patient discharge instructions completeness and performance on a national quality measure: A quasi-experimental study. *Applied Clinical Informatics* 4(4):499-515.

Bell, R. M., and Y. Koren. 2007. *Scalable collaborative filtering with jointly derived neighborhood interpolation weights.* Paper presented at Seventh IEEE International Conference on Data Mining, Omaha, NE.

Bergeson, S. C., and J. D. Dean. 2006. A systems approach to patient-centered care. *JAMA* 296(23):2848-2851.

Berry, L. L., D. Beckham, A. Dettman, and R. Mead. 2014. Toward a strategy of patient-centered access to primary care. *Mayo Clinic Proceedings* 89(10):1406-1415.

Bisgaier, J., and K. V. Rhodes. 2011. Auditing access to specialty care for children with public insurance. *New England Journal of Medicine* 364(24):2324-2333.

Bisgaier, J., D. Polsky, and K. V. Rhodes. 2012. Academic medical centers and equity in specialty care access for children. *Archives of Pediatrics and Adolescent Medicine* 166(4):304-310.

Blackmore, C. C., R. S. Mecklenburg, and G. S. Kaplan. 2011. At Virginia Mason, collaboration among providers, employers, and health plans to transform care cut costs and improved quality. *Health Affairs* 30(9):1680-1687.

Bleustein, C., D. B. Rothschild, A. Valen, E. Valatis, L. Schweitzer, and R. Jones. 2014. Wait times, patient satisfaction scores, and the perception of care. *American Journal of Managed Care* 20(5):393-400.

Blumenthal, D., and C. M. Kilo. 1998. A report card on continuous quality improvement. *Milbank Quarterly* 76(4):625-648.

Bodenheimer, T. 2008. Coordinating care—a perilous journey through the health care system. *New England Journal of Medicine* 358(10):1064-1071.

Bodenheimer, T., E. Chen, and H. D. Bennett. 2009. Confronting the growing burden of chronic disease: Can the U.S. Health care workforce do the job? *Health Affairs* 28(1):64-74.

Boisjoly, H., E. E. Freeman, F. Djafari, M.-J. Aubin, S. Couture, R. P. Bruen, R. Gizicki, and J. Gresset. 2010. Reducing wait time for cataract surgery: Comparison of 2 historical cohorts of patients in Montreal. *Canadian Journal of Ophthalmology/Journal Canadien d'Ophtalmologie* 45(2):135-139.

Borchard, A., D. L. B. Schwappach, A. Barbir, and P. Bezzola. 2012. A systematic review of the effectiveness, compliance, and critical factors for implementation of safety checklists in surgery. *Annals of Surgery* 256(6):925-933.

Brandenburg, L., P. A. Gabow, W. C. Rupp, G. D. Steele, Jr., J. S. Toussaint, and B. Tyson. 2015. Innovation and best practices in health care scheduling. Washington, DC. http://www.iom.edu/Global/Perspectives/2015/Innovation-and-Best-Practices-in-Health-Care-Scheduling.aspx (accessed April 22, 2015).

Braybrooke, J., H. Ahn, A. Gallant, M. Ford, Y. Bronstein, J. Finkelstein, and A. Yee. 2007. The impact of surgical wait time on patient-based outcomes in posterior lumbar spinal surgery. *European Spine Journal* 16(11):1832-1839.

Brousseau, D. C., J. Bergholte, and M. H. Gorelick. 2004. The effect of prior interactions with a primary care provider on nonurgent pediatric emergency department use. *Archives of Pediatrics & Adolescent Medicine* 158(1):78-82.

Bureau of Labor Statistics. 2013. *Occupations with the largest projected number of job openings due to growth and replacement needs, 2012 and projected 2022.* http://www.bls.gov/news.release/ecopro.t08.htm (accessed May 1, 2015).

Carman, K. L., P. Dardess, M. Maurer, S. Sofaer, K. Adams, C. Bechtel, and J. Sweeney. 2013. Patient and family engagement: A framework for understanding the elements and developing interventions and policies. *Health Affairs* 32(2):223-231.

Cesena, F. H. Y., D. Favarato, L. A. M. César, S. A. de Oliveira, and P. L. da Luz. 2004. Cardiac complications during waiting for elective coronary artery bypass graft surgery: Incidence, temporal distribution and predictive factors. *European Journal of Cardio-Thoracic Surgery* 25(2):196-202.

REFERENCES

Charles, B. L. 2000. Telemedicine can lower costs and improve access. *Healthcare Finance Management* 54(4):66-69.

Chen, F. 2001. Market segmentation, advanced demand information, and supply chain performance. *Manufacturing & Service Operations Management* 3(1):53-67.

Christensen, E. D., T. Harvald, M. Jendresen, S. Aggestrup, and G. Petterson. 1997. The impact of delayed diagnosis of lung cancer on the stage at the time of operation. *European Journal of Cardio-Thoracic Surgery* 12(6):880-884.

Cima, R. R., M. J. Brown, J. R. Hebl, R. Moore, J. C. Rogers, A. Kollengode, G. J. Amstutz, C. A. Weisbrod, B. J. Narr, and C. Deschamps. 2011. Use of Lean and Six Sigma methodology to improve operating room efficiency in a high-volume tertiary-care academic medical center. *Journal of the American College of Surgeons* 213(1):83-92.

CMS (Centers for Medicare & Medicaid Services). 2015a. *About CMS.* http://www.cms.gov/About-CMS/About-CMS.html (accessed May 1, 2015).

———. 2015b. *Centers for Medicare & Medicaid Services partnership for patients.* http://partnershipforpatients.cms.gov/about-the-partnership/aboutthepartnershipforpatients.html (accessed March 16, 2015).

———. 2015c. *CMs innovation center.* http://innovation.cms.gov (accessed March 16, 2015).

———. 2015d. *CY2016 MA HSD Provider and facility specialties and network adequacy criteria guidance.* http://www.cms.gov/Medicare/Medicare-Advantage/MedicareAdvantageApps/Downloads/CY2015_MA_HSD_Network_Criteria_Guidance.pdf (accessed March 16, 2015).

———. 2015e. *Health care innovation awards round two: Econsults/ereferrals: Controlling costs and improving quality at the interface of primary care and specialty care.* http://innovation.cms.gov/initiatives/Participant/Health-Care-Innovation-Awards-Round-Two/Association-Of-American-Medical-Colleges.html (accessed March 16, 2015).

Coates, A. S. 1999. Breast cancer: Delays, dilemmas, and delusions. *Lancet* 353(9159):1112-1113.

Coats, T., and S. Michalis. 2001. Mathematical modelling of patient flow through an accident and emergency department. *Emergency Medicine Journal* 18(3):190-192.

Coleman, E. A., J. D. Smith, J. C. Frank, S.-J. Min, C. Parry, and A. M. Kramer. 2004. Preparing patients and caregivers to participate in care delivered across settings: The care transitions intervention. *Journal of the American Geriatric Society* 52(11):1817-1825.

Coleman, E. A., C. Parry, S. Chalmers, and S. Min. 2006. The care transitions intervention: Results of a randomized controlled trial. *Archives of Internal Medicine* 166(17):1822-1828.

Conner-Spady, B., C. Sanmartin, S. Sanmugasunderam, C. De Coster, D. Lorenzetti, L. McLaren, J. McGurran, and T. Noseworthy. 2007. A systematic literature review of the evidence on benchmarks for cataract surgery waiting time. *Canadian Journal of Ophthalmology/Journal Canadien d'Ophtalmologie* 42(4):543-551.

Cooper, G. E., M. D. White, and J. K. Lauber. 1980. *Resource management on the flight deck.* Edited by G. E. Cooper, M. D. White and J. K. Lauber, Proceedings of a NASA/industry workshop, San Francisco, 26-28 June. 1979. San Francisco, CA.

Council, M. H. 2014. *Annual report on the performance of the Massachusetts health care system.* Boston, MA: Center for Health Informatics and Analysis.

Darkins, A., P. Ryan, R. Kobb, L. Foster, E. Edmonson, B. Wakefield, and A. E. Lancaster. 2008. Care coordination/home telehealth: The systematic implementation of health informatics, home telehealth, and disease management to support the care of veteran patients with chronic conditions. *Telemedicine and e-Health* 14(10):1118-1126.

Davis, K., S. C. Schoenbaum, and A. M. Audet. 2005. A 2020 vision of patient-centered primary care. *Journal of General Internal Medicine* 20(10):953-957.

Davis, R. E., R. Jacklin, N. Sevdalis, and C. A. Vincent. 2007. Patient involvement in patient safety: What factors influence patient participation and engagement? *Health Expectations* 10(3):259-267.

Desalvo, K. B., B. E. Bowdish, A. S. Alper, D. M. Grossman, and W. W. Merrill. 2000. Physician practice variation in assignment of return interval. *Archives of Internal Medicine* 160(2):205-208.

Desmeules, F., C. E. Dionne, É. L. Belzile, R. Bourbonnais, and P. Frémont. 2012. The impacts of pre-surgery wait for total knee replacement on pain, function and health-related quality of life six months after surgery. *Journal of Evaluation in Clinical Practice* 18(1):111-120.

Devaraj, S., T. T. Ow, and R. Kohli. 2013. Examining the impact of information technology and patient flow on healthcare performance: A theory of swift and even flow (TSEF) perspective. *Journal of Operations Management* 31(4):181-192.

Dhar, S., R. Michel, and B. Kanna. 2011. Improving visit cycle time using patient flow analysis in a high-volume inner-city hospital-based ambulatory clinic serving minority New Yorkers. *Journal for Healthcare Quality* 33(2):23-28.

DiGioia, A., H. Lorenz, P. K. Greenhouse, D. A. Bertoty, and S. D. Rocks. 2010. A patient-centered model to improve metrics without cost increase viewing all care through the eyes of patients and families. *Journal of Nursing Administration* 40(12):540-546.

Dobson, I., Q. Doan, and G. Hung. 2013. A systematic review of patient tracking systems for use in the pediatric emergency department. *Journal of Emergency Medicine* 44(1):242-248.

DoD (Department of Defense). 2014. *Military health system review*. Washington, DC: Department of Defense.

Edwards, P. J., D. T. Huang, L. N. Metcalfe, and F. Sainfort. 2008. Maximizing your investment in EHR. Utilizing EHRs to inform continuous quality improvement. *Journal of Healthcare Information Management* 22(1):32-37.

Evangelista, J. A., J. A. Connor, C. Pintz, T. Saia, C. O'Connell, D. R. Fulton, and P. Hickey. 2012. Paediatric nurse practitioner managed cardiology clinics: Patient satisfaction and appointment access. *Journal of Advanced Nursing* 68(10):2165-2174.

Evans, J., and W. Lindsay. 2015. *An introduction to Six Sigma and process improvement*. 2nd ed. Stamford, CT: CENGAGE Learning.

Everett, J. E. 2002. A decision support simulation model for the management of an elective surgery waiting system. *Health Care Management Science* 5(2):89-95.

Gabow, P. A., and P. L. Goodman. 2014. *The Lean prescription: Powerful medicine for our ailing healthcare system*. New York: Productivity Press.

Gallucci, G., W. Swartz, and F. Hackerman. 2005. Impact of the wait for an initial appointment on the rate of kept appointments at a mental health center. *Psychiatric Services* 56(3):344-346.

Garbuz, D. S., M. Xu, C. P. Duncan, B. A. Masri, and B. Sobolev. 2006. Delays worsen quality of life outcome of primary total hip arthroplasty. *Clinical Orthopaedics and Related Research* 447:79-84.

Gayed, B., S. Black, J. Daggy, and I. A. Munshi. 2013. Redesigning a joint replacement program using Lean Six Sigma in a Veterans Affairs hospital. *JAMA Surgery* 148(11):1050-1056.

Gong, B., D. Muhlestein, A. Choudhri, and J. Slackman. 2015. *The impact of accountable care: Health insurers and the accountable care movement*. Princeton, NJ: Robert Wood Johnson Foundation.

Graban, M. 2012. *Lean hospitals : Improving quality, patient safety, and employee engagement*. 2nd ed. New York: Productivity Press/Taylor & Francis.

Grumbach, K. 2009. Redesign of the health care delivery system: A Bauhaus "form follows function" approach. *JAMA* 302(21):2363-2364.

Grumbach, K., and T. Bodenheimer. 2004. Can health care teams improve primary care practice? *JAMA* 291(10):1246-1251.

Guttmann, A., M. J. Schull, M. J. Vermeulen, and T. A. Stukel. 2011. Association between waiting times and short term mortality and hospital admission after departure from emergency department: Population based cohort study from Ontario, Canada. *BMJ* 342:d2983.

Hagan, P. 2011. Waste not, want not: Leading the Lean health-care journey at Seattle Children's Hospital. *Global Business and Organizational Excellence* 30(3):25-31.

Haggarty, J. M., J. A. Jarva, Z. Cernovsky, K. Karioja, and L. Martin. 2012. Wait time impact of co-located primary care mental health services: The effect of adding collaborative care in northern Ontario. *Canadian Journal of Psychiatry* 57(1):29.

Hall, R. 2012. Matching healthcare resources to patient needs. In *Handbook of healthcare system scheduling*, edited by R. Hall. New York: Springer Science and Business Media.

———. 2013. *Patient flow: Reducing delay in healthcare delivery*. New York: Springer Science & Business Media.

Hall, R., D. Belson, P. Murali, and M. Dessouky. 2013. Modeling patient flows through the healthcare system. In *Patient flow: reducing delay in healthcare delivery, Vol. 206*, edited by R. Hall. New York: Springer Science and Business Media.

Harry, M. J. 1998. Six Sigma: A breakthrough strategy for profitability. *Quality Progress* 31(5):60-64.

Haynes, A. B., T. G. Weiser, W. R. Berry, S. R. Lipsitz, A. H. S. Breizat, E. P. Dellinger, T. Herbosa, S. Joseph, P. L. Kibatala, M. C. M. Lapitan, A. F. Merry, K. Moorthy, R. K. Reznick, B. Taylor, and A. A. Gawande. 2009. A surgical safety checklist to reduce morbidity and mortality in a global population. *New England Journal of Medicine* 360(5):491-499.

HHS (Department of Health and Human Services). 2015. *HITECH Act enforcement interim final rule*. http://www.hhs.gov/ocr/privacy/hipaa/administrative/enforcementrule/hitechenforcementifr.html (accessed May 1, 2015).

Hibbard, J. H., and J. Greene. 2013. What the evidence shows about patient activation: Better health outcomes and care experiences; fewer data on costs. *Health Affairs* 32(2):207-214.

Hirvonen, J., M. Blom, U. Tuominen, S. Seitsalo, M. Lehto, P. Paavolainen, K. Hietaniemi, P. Rissanen, and H. Sintonen. 2007. Evaluating waiting time effect on health outcomes at admission: A prospective randomized study on patients with osteoarthritis of the knee joint. *Journal of Evaluation in Clinical Practice* 13(5):728-733.

Hodge, W., T. Horsley, D. Albiani, J. Baryla, M. Belliveau, R. Buhrmann, M. O'Connor, J. Blair, and E. Lowcock. 2007. The consequences of waiting for cataract surgery: A systematic review. *Canadian Medical Association Journal* 176(9):1285-1290.

Hoffman, K. A., A. Quanbeck, J. H. Ford, 2nd, F. Wrede, D. Wright, D. Lambert-Wacey, P. Chvojka, A. Hanchett, and D. McCarty. 2011. Improving substance abuse data systems to measure "waiting time to treatment": Lessons learned from a quality improvement initiative. *Health Informatics Journal* 17(4):256-265.

Holden, R. J. 2011. Lean thinking in emergency departments: A critical review. *Annals of Emergency Medicine* 57(3):265-278.

Holweg, M. 2007. The genealogy of Lean production. *Journal of Operations Management* 25(2):420-437.

Hoot, N. R., and D. Aronsky. 2008. Systematic review of emergency department crowding: Causes, effects, and solutions. *Annals of Emergency Medicine* 52(2):126-136.

Howley, M. J., E. Y. Chou, N. Hansen, and P. W. Dalrymple. 2015. The long-term financial impact of electronic health record implementation. *Journal of the American Medical Informatics Association* 22(2):443-452.

HRSA (Health Resources and Services Administration). 2015. *About HRSA*. http://www.hrsa.gov/about/index.html (accessed May 7, 2015).

Hsu, C., K. Coleman, T. R. Ross, E. Johnson, P. A. Fishman, E. B. Larson, D. Liss, C. Trescott, and R. J. Reid. 2012. Spreading a patient-centered medical home redesign: A case study. *Journal of Ambulatory Care Management* 35(2):99-108.

Huges, R. G. 2008. Chapter 44: Tools and strategies for quality improvement and patient safety. In *Patient safety and quality: An evidence-based handbook for nurses*. Rockville, MD: AHRQ.

Hughes, G. 2010. Four hour target for EDs: The UK experience. *Emergency Medicine Australasia* 22(5):368-373.

Hwang, A. H., M. M. Hwang, H. W. Xie, B. E. Hardy, and D. L. Skaggs. 2005. Access to urologic care for children in California: Medicaid versus private insurance. *Urology* 66(1):170-173.

IHI (Institute for Healthcare Improvement). 2003. *Optimizing patient flow: Moving patients smoothly through acute care settings*. Cambridge, MA: Institute for Healthcare Improvement.

———. 2014a. *Office visit cycle time*. http://www.ihi.resources/Pages/Measures/OfficeVisitCycleTime.aspx (accessed October 14, 2014).

———. 2014b. *Third next available appointment*. http://www.ihi.org/resources/Pages/Measures/ThirdNextAvailableAppointment.aspx (accessed October 14, 2014).

IHO (Institute for Healthcare Optimization). 2015. *IHO Variability Methodology® services*. http://www.ihoptimize.org/what-we-do-methodology.htm (accessed April, 27, 2015).

IOM (Institute of Medicine). 2000. *To err is human: Building a safer health system*. Edited by L. T. Kohn, J. M. Corrigan, and M. S. Donaldson. Washington, DC: National Academy Press.

———. 2001a. *Crossing the quality chasm: A new health system for the 21st century*. Washington, DC: National Academy Press.

———. 2001b. *Finding what works in health care: Standards for systematic reviews*. Washington, DC: National Academy Press.

———. 2011. *The future of nursing: Leading change, advancing health*. Washington, DC: The National Academies Press.

———. 2012. *The role of telehealth in an evolving health care environment: Workshop summary*. Washington, DC: The National Academies Press.

———. 2013. *Best care at lower cost: The path to continuously learning health care in America*. Washington, DC: The National Academies Press.

———. 2015. *Engineering optimal health care scheduling: Perspectives for the nation: Workshop in brief*. Washington, DC: Institute of Medicine.

Jack, B. W., V. K. Chetty, D. Anthony, J. L. Greenwald, G. M. Sanchez, A. E. Johnson, S. R. Forsythe, J. K. O'Donnell, M. K. Paasche-Orlow, C. Manasseh, S. Martin, and L. Culpepper. 2009. A reengineered hospital discharge program to decrease rehospitalization: A randomized trial. *Annals of Internal Medicine* 150(3):178-187.

JC (The Joint Commission). 2015. *Facts about The Joint Commission*. http://www.jointcommission.org/facts_about_the_joint_commission (accessed May 1, 2015).

Jennings, B. M. 2008. Patient acuity. In *Patient safety and quality: An evidence-based handbook for nurses*, edited by R. G. Hughes. Rockville, MD: AHRQ.

JHU (Johns Hopkins University). 2015. *Tertiary care definition*. http://www.hopkinsmedicine.org/patient_care/pay_bill/insurance_footnotes.html (accessed March 14, 2015).

Johnson, M., S. Myers, J. Wineholt, M. Pollack, and A. L. Kusmiesz. 2009. Patients who leave the emergency department without being seen. *Journal of Emergency Nursing* 35(2):105-108.

Jones, P., and K. Schimanski. 2010. The four hour target to reduce emergency department "waiting time": A systematic review of clinical outcomes. *Emergency Medicine Australasia* 22(5):391-398.

REFERENCES

Jones, S. S., and R. S. Evans. 2008. *An agent based simulation tool for scheduling emergency department physicians.* Paper read at AMIA Annual Symposium, Washington, DC.

Jweinat, J., P. Damore, V. Morris, R. D'Aquila, S. Bacon, and T. J. Balcezak. 2013. The safe patient flow initiative: A collaborative quality improvement journey at Yale-New Haven Hospital. *The Joint Commission Journal on Quality and Patient Safety* 39(10):447-459.

Kabcenell, A., and K. Luther. 2012. Creating a culture of excellence. It's not as difficult as you might think. *Healthcare Executive* 27(4):68, 70-71.

Kaplan, G., G. Bo-Linn, P. Carayon, P. Pronovost, W. Rouse, P. Reid, and R. Saunders. 2013. Bringing a systems approach to health. Washington, DC. http://www.iom.edu/Global/Perspectives/2013/SystemsApproaches.aspx (accessed April 22, 2015).

Kehle, S. M., N. Greer, I. Rutks, and T. Wilt. 2011. Interventions to improve veterans' access to care: A systematic review of the literature. *Journal of General Internal Medicine* 26(Suppl 2):689-696.

Kenter, R., L. Warmerdam, C. Brouwer-Dudokdewit, P. Cuijpers, and A. van Straten. 2013. Guided online treatment in routine mental health care: An observational study on uptake, drop-out and effects. *BMC Psychiatry* 13:43.

KFF (Kaiser Family Foundation). 2015. *The coverage gap: Uninsured poor adults in states that do not expand Medicaid—an update.* Washington, DC: Kaiser Family Foundation.

Kim, C. S., D. A. Spahlinger, J. M. Kin, and J. E. Billi. 2006. Lean health care: What can hospitals learn from a world-class automaker? *Journal of Hospital Medicine* 1(3):191-199.

Kim, C. S., D. A. Spahlinger, and J. E. Billi. 2009. Creating value in health care: The case for Lean thinking. *Journal of Clinical Outcomes Management* 16(12):557-562.

Kolker, A. 2008. Process modeling of emergency department patient flow: Effect of patient length of stay on ED diversion. *Journal of Medical Systems* 32(5):389-401.

Krier, D., and T. Thompson. 2014 (unpublished). *Engineering optimal health care scheduling: Presentation.* Cincinnati Children's Hospital.

Kwak, Y. H., and F. T. Anbari. 2006. Benefits, obstacles, and future of Six Sigma approach. *Technovation* 26(5-6):708-715.

Lake, T., C. Kvam, and M. Gold. 2005. *Literature review: Using quality information for health care decisions and quality improvement* Cambridge, MA: Mathematica Policy Research, Inc.

Lamb, G., R. Tappen, S. Diaz, L. Herndon, and J. G. Ouslander. 2011. Avoidability of hospital transfers of nursing home residents: Perspectives of frontline staff. *Journal of the American Geriatrics Society* 59(9):1665-1672.

Leape, L., D. Berwick, C. Clancy, J. Conway, P. Gluck, J. Guest, D. Lawrence, J. Morath, D. O'Leary, P. O'Neill, D. Pinakiewicz, and T. Isaac. 2009. Transforming healthcare: A safety imperative. *Quality and Safety in Health Care* 18(6):424-428.

Leddy, K. M., D. O. Kaldenberg, and B. W. Becker. 2003. Timeliness in ambulatory care treatment. An examination of patient satisfaction and wait times in medical practices and outpatient test and treatment facilities. *Journal of Ambulatory Care Management* 26(2):138-149.

Lee, E. K., H. Y. Atallah, M. D. Wright, E. T. Post, C. Thomas, D. T. Wu, and L. L. Haley. 2015. Transforming hospital emergency department workflow and patient care. *Interfaces* 45(1):58-82.

Levinson, D. R. 2014. *Access to care: Provider availability in Medicaid managed care.* http://oig.hhs.gov/oei/reports/oei-02-13-00670.pdf (accessed July 29, 2015).

Lingard, L., G. Regehr, B. Orser, R. Reznick, G. R. Baker, D. Doran, S. Espin, J. Bohnen, and S. Whyte. 2008. Evaluation of a preoperative checklist and team briefing among surgeons, nurses, and anesthesiologists to reduce failures in communication. *Archives of Surgery* 143(1):12-17.

Litvak, E. 2009. *Managing patient flow in hospitals: Strategies and solutions.* Oak Brook, IL: Joint Commission Resources, Inc.

———. 2015. Outpatient and primary care clinic: St. Thomas Community Health Center, New Orleans, LA. http://ihoptimize.com (accessed January 28, 2015).

Litvak, E., and M. Bisognano. 2011. More patients, less payment: Increasing hospital efficiency in the aftermath of health reform. *Health Affairs* 30(1):76-80.

Litvak, E., and H. V. Fineberg. 2013. Smoothing the way to high quality, safety, and economy. *New England Journal of Medicine* 369(17):1581-1583.

Litvak, E., and M. C. Long. 2000. Cost and quality under managed care: Irreconcilable differences? *American Journal of Managed Care* 6(3):305-312.

Liu, S. S., and J. Chen. 2009. Using data mining to segment healthcare markets from patients' preference perspectives. *International Journal of Health Care Quality Assurance* 22(2):117-134.

Llanwarne, N. R., G. A. Abel, M. N. Elliott, C. A. M. Paddison, G. Lyratzopoulos, J. L. Campbell, and M. Roland. 2013. Relationship between clinical quality and patient experience: Analysis of data from the English quality and outcomes framework and the national General Practice Patient Survey. *Annals of Family Medicine* 11(5):467-472.

Longtin, Y., H. Sax, L. L. Leape, S. E. Sheridan, L. Donaldson, and D. Pittet. 2010. Patient participation: Current knowledge and applicability to patient safety. *Mayo Clinic Proceedings* 85(1):53-62.

Martin, G. P., and R. Finn. 2011. Patients as team members: Opportunities, challenges and paradoxes of including patients in multi-professional healthcare teams. *Sociology of Health & Illness* 33(7):1050-1065.

Mazzocato, P., C. Savage, M. Brommels, H. Aronsson, and J. Thor. 2010. Lean thinking in healthcare: A realist review of the literature. *Quality and Safety in Health Care* 19(5):376-382.

McGowan, J. J., C. M. Cusack, and M. Bloomrosen. 2012. The future of health IT innovation and informatics: A report from AMIA's 2010 policy meeting. *Journal of the American Medical Informatics Association* 19(3):460-467.

Melon, K. A., D. White, and J. Rankin. 2013. Beat the clock! Wait times and the production of "quality" in emergency departments. *Nursing Philosophy* 14(3):223-237.

Merrick, N. J., R. Houchens, S. Tillisch, B. Berlow, and C. Landon. 2001. Quality of hospital care of children with asthma: Medicaid versus privately insured patients. *Journal of Health Care for the Poor and Underserved* 12(2):192-207.

MerrittHawkins. 2014. *Physician appointment wait times and Medicaid and Medicare acceptance rates.* Irvine, TX: MerrittHawkins.

Meyer, H. 2011. At UPMC, improving care processes to serve patients better and cut costs. *Health Affairs* 30(3):400-403.

Meyer, W. 2001. Why they don't come back: A clinical perspective on the no-show client. *Clinical Social Work Journal* 29(4):325-339.

Michael, M., S. D. Schaffer, P. L. Egan, B. B. Little, and P. S. Pritchard. 2013. Improving wait times and patient satisfaction in primary care. *Journal for Healthcare Quality* 35(2):50-59; quiz 59-60.

MMS (Massachusetts Medical Society). 2013. *2013 MMS patient access to care study.* Waltham, MA: Massachusetts Medical Society.

Moja, L., A. Piatti, V. Pecoraro, C. Ricci, G. Virgili, G. Salanti, L. Germagnoli, A. Liberati, and G. Banfi. 2012. Timing matters in hip fracture surgery: Patients operated within 48 hours have better outcomes. A meta-analysis and meta-regression of over 190,000 patients. *PLoS ONE* 7(10):e46175.

Montebello, A. R. 1994. Teamwork in health care: Opportunities for gains in quality, productivity, and competitive advantage. What works, what doesn't, and why. *Clinical Laboratory Management Review* 8(2):91-105.

Monzon, J., S. M. Friedman, C. Clarke, and T. Arenovich. 2005. Patients who leave the emergency department without being seen by a physician: A control-matched study. *Canadian Journal of Emergency Medicine* 7(2):107-113.

Murray, M. 2002. Reducing waits and delays in the referral process. *Family Practice Management* 9(3):39-42.

Murray, M., and D. M. Berwick. 2003. Advanced access. *JAMA* 289(8):1035-1040.

Murray, M., T. Bodenheimer, D. Rittenhouse, and K. Grumbach. 2003. Improving timely access to primary care: Case studies of the advanced access model. *JAMA* 289(8):1042-1046.

Murray, M., M. Davies, and B. Boushon. 2007. Panel size: How many patients can one doctor manage? *Family Practice Management* 14(4):44-51.

Murrin, S. 2014. *State standards for access to care in Medicaid managed care.* http://oig.hhs.gov/oei/reports/oei-02-11-00320.pdf (accessed April 22, 2015).

NAE (National Academy of Engineering) and IOM (Institute of Medicine). 2005. *Building a better delivery system: A new engineering/health care partnership.* Washington, DC: The National Academies Press.

Naylor, C., and C. Imison. 2010. Referral management. Rational ways to rein in referrals. *Health Services Journal* 120(6230):22-23.

NCQA (National Committee for Quality Assurance). 2015. *About NCQA.* http://www.ncqa.org/AboutNCQA.aspx (accessed May 1, 2015).

Neily, J., P. D. Mills, Y. N. Young-Xu, B. T. Carney, P. West, D. H. Berger, L. M. Mazzia, D. E. Paull, and J. P. Bagian. 2010. Association between implementation of a medical team training program and surgical mortality. *JAMA* 304(15):1693-1700.

Nelson, K. M., C. Helfrich, H. L. Sun, P. L. Hebert, C. F. Liu, E. Dolan, L. Taylor, E. Wong, C. Maynard, S. E. Hernandez, W. Sanders, I. Randall, I. Curtis, G. Schectman, R. Stark, and S. D. Fihn. 2014. Implementation of the patient-centered medical home in the Veterans Health Administration: Associations with patient satisfaction, quality of care, staff burnout, and hospital and emergency department use. *JAMA Internal Medicine* 174(8):1350-1358.

Nelson-Peterson, D. L., and C. J. Leppa. 2007. Creating an environment for caring using Lean principles of the Virginia Mason production system. *Journal of Nursing Administration* 37(6):287-294.

NQF (National Quality Forum). 2015. *The National Quality Forum: About us.* http://www.qualityforum.org/story/About_Us.aspx (accessed May 1, 2015).

O'Hagan, J., and D. Persaud. 2009. Creating a culture of accountability in health care. *Health Care Manag (Frederick)* 28(2):124-133.

ONC (Office of the National Coordinator for Healh Information Technology). 2015. *About ONC.* http://www.healthit.gov/newsroom/about-onc (accessed May 7, 2015).

Oredsson, S., H. Jonsson, J. Rognes, L. Lind, K. E. Goransson, A. Ehrenberg, K. Asplund, M. Castren, and N. Farrohknia. 2011. A systematic review of triage-related interventions to improve patient flow in emergency departments. *Scandinavian Journal of Trauma Resuscitation and Emergency Medicine* 19:43.

Paccagnella, A., A. Mauri, and N. Spinella. 2012. Quality improvement for integrated management of patients with type 2 diabetes (PRIHTA project stage 1). *Quality Management in Health Care* 21(3):146-159.

Passalent, L. A., C. Kennedy, K. Warmington, L. J. Soever, K. Lundon, R. Shupak, S. Lineker, and R. Schneider. 2013. System integration and clinical utilization of the advanced clinician practitioner in arthritis care (ACPAC) program-trained extended role practitioners in ontario: A two-year, system-level evaluation. *Healthcare Policy* 8(4):56-70.

Paterson, W. G., W. T. Depew, P. Paré, D. Petrunia, C. Switzer, S. J. V. van Zanten, and S. Daniels. 2006. Canadian consensus on medically acceptable wait times for digestive health care. *Canadian Journal of Gastroenterology* 20(6):411-423.

Pearl, R. 2014. Kaiser Permanente Northern California: Current experiences with Internet, mobile, and video technologies. *Health Affairs* 33(2):251-257.

Petterson, S. M., R. L. J. Phillips, A. W. Bazemore, and G. T. Koinis. 2013. Unequal distribution of the U.S. primary care workforce. *American Family Physician* 87(11). http://www.aafp.org/afp/2013/0601/od1.html (accessed April 22, 2015).

Pizer, S. D., and J. C. Prentice. 2011a. Time is money: Outpatient waiting times and health insurance choices of elderly veterans in the United States. *Journal of Health Economics* 30(4):626-636.

———. 2011b. What are the consequences of waiting for health care in the veteran population? *Journal of General Internal Medicine* 26:S676-S682.

Prasanna, M., and V. Sekar. 2013. Lean Six Sigma in SMES: An exploration through literature review. *Journal of Engineering, Design and Technology* 11(3):224-250.

Prentice, J. C., and S. D. Pizer. 2007. Delayed access to health care and mortality. *Health Services Research* 42(2):644-662.

Pronovost, P., D. Needham, S. Berenholtz, D. Sinopoli, H. Chu, S. Cosgrove, B. Sexton, R. Hyzy, R. Welsh, G. Roth, J. Bander, J. Kepros, and C. Goeschel. 2006. An intervention to decrease catheter-related bloodstream infections in the ICU. *New England Journal of Medicine* 355(26):2725-2732.

Reid, R. J., P. A. Fishman, O. Yu, T. R. Ross, J. T. Tufano, M. P. Soman, and E. B. Larson. 2009. Patient-centered medical home demonstration: A prospective, quasi-experimental, before and after evaluation. *American Journal of Managed Care* 15(9):71-87.

Reid, R. J., K. Coleman, E. A. Johnson, P. A. Fishman, C. Hsu, Michael P. Soman, C. E. Trescott, M. Erikson, and E. B. Larson. 2010. The group health medical home at year two: Cost savings, higher patient satisfaction, and less burnout for providers. *Health Affairs* 29(5):835-843.

Reid, R. J., E. A. Johnson, C. Hsu, K. Ehrlich, K. Coleman, C. Trescott, M. Erikson, T. R. Ross, D. T. Liss, D. Cromp, P. A. Fishman. 2013. Spreading a medical home redesign: Effects on Emergency Room Use and Hospital Admissions. *Annals of Family Medicine* 11(1 Supp):S19-S26.

Rhodes, K. V., G. M. Kenney, A. B. Friedman, B. Saloner, C. C. Lawson, D. Chearo, D. Wissoker, and D. Polsky. 2014. Primary care access for new patients on the eve of health care reform. *JAMA Internal Medicine* 174(6):861-869.

Rickard, M. 2015. St. Thomas fills health care need in community. *The New Orleans Advocate*, February 4, 2015.

Rose, K. D., J. S. Ross, and L. I. Horwitz. 2011. Advanced access scheduling outcomes: A systematic review. *Archives of Internal Medicine* 171(13):1150-1159.

Ryckman, F. C., P. A. Yelton, A. M. Anneken, P. E. Kiessling, P. J. Schoettker, and U. R. Kotagal. 2009. Redesigning intensive care unit flow using variability management to improve access and safety. *Joint Commission Journal on Quality and Patient Safety* 35(11):535-543.

Saaty, T. L. 1961. *Elements of queueing theory*. Vol. 423. New York: McGraw-Hill.

Savage, I. 2013. Comparing the fatality risks in United States transportation across modes and over time. *Research in Transportation Economics* 43(1):9-22.

Schneider, E. C., A. M. Zaslavsky, B. E. Landon, T. R. Lied, S. Sheingold, and P. D. Cleary. 2001. National quality monitoring of Medicare health plans: The relationship between enrollees' reports and the quality of clinical care. *Medical Care* 39(12):1313-1325.

Schroeder, R. G., K. Linderman, C. Liedtke, and A. S. Choo. 2008. Six Sigma: Definition and underlying theory. *Journal of Operations Management* 26(4):536-554.

Simunovic, N., P. J. Devereaux, S. Sprague, G. H. Guyatt, E. Schemitsch, J. DeBeer, and M. Bhandari. 2010. Effect of early surgery after hip fracture on mortality and complications: Systematic review and meta-analysis. *Canadian Medical Association Journal* 182(15):1609-1616.

Sirovich, B., P. M. Gallagher, D. E. Wennberg, and E. S. Fisher. 2008. Discretionary decision making by primary care physicians and the cost of U.S. health care. *Health Affairs (Millwood)* 27(3):813-823.

Smart, N. A., and T. T. Titus. 2011. Outcomes of early versus late nephrology referral in chronic kidney disease: A systematic review. *American Journal of Medicine* 124(11):1073-1080.e1072.

Smektala, R., H. G. Endres, B. Dasch, C. Maier, H. J. Trampisch, F. Bonnaire, and L. Pientka. 2008. The effect of time-to-surgery on outcome in elderly patients with proximal femoral fractures. *BMC Musculoskeletal Disorders* 9:171.

Smith, C. D., T. Spackman, K. Brommer, M. W. Stewart, M. Vizzini, J. Frye, and W. C. Rupp. 2013. Re-engineering the operating room using variability methodology to improve health care value. *Journal of the American College of Surgeons* 216(4):559-568.

Sobolev, B., L. Kuramoto, A. Levy, and R. Hayden. 2006a. Methods for studying adverse events on surgical wait lists. *Health Services and Outcomes Research Methodology* 6(3-4):139-151.

Sobolev, B. G., A. R. Levy, L. Kuramoto, R. Hayden, and J. M. FitzGerald. 2006b. Do longer delays for coronary artery bypass surgery contribute to preoperative mortality in less urgent patients? *Medical Care* 44(7):680-686.

Sobolev, B. G., G. Fradet, L. Kuramoto, and B. Rogula. 2012. An observational study to evaluate 2 target times for elective coronary bypass surgery. *Medical Care* 50(7):611-619.

———. 2013. The occurrence of adverse events in relation to time after registration for coronary artery bypass surgery: A population-based observational study. *Journal of Cardiothoracic Surgery* 8:74.

Stainsby, H., M. Taboada, and E. Luque. 2009. *Towards an agent-based simulation of hospital emergency departments.* Paper presented at IEEE International Conference on Services Computing, Bangalore, India.

Stapleton, F. B., J. Hendricks, P. Hagan, and M. DelBeccaro. 2009. Modifying the Toyota production system for continuous performance improvement in an academic children's hospital. *Pediatric Clinics of North America* 56(4):799.

Steinbauer, J. R., K. Korell, J. Erdin, and S. J. Spann. 2006. Implementing open-access scheduling in an academic practice. *Family Practice Management* 13(3):59-64.

Tanne, J. H. 2010. More U.S. doctors are refusing to accept government insured patients. *BMJ* 340:c3476.

Taylor, M. J., C. McNicholas, C. Nicolay, A. Darzi, D. Bell, and J. E. Reed. 2013. Systematic review of the application of the plan–do–study–act method to improve quality in healthcare. *BMJ Quality & Safety.* http://qualitysafety.bmj.com/content/early/2013/09/11/bmjqs-2013-001862.full (accessed April 22, 2015).

Thompson, D. A., P. R. Yarnold, D. R. Williams, and S. L. Adams. 1996. Effects of actual waiting time, perceived waiting time, information delivery, and expressive quality on patient satisfaction in the emergency department. *Annals of Emergency Medicine* 28(6):657-665.

Toussaint, J. S., and L. L. Berry. 2013. The promise of Lean in health care. *Mayo Clin Proc* 88(1):74-82.

Trastek, V. F., N. W. Hamilton, and E. E. Niles. 2014. Leadership models in health care—a case for servant leadership. *Mayo Clinic Proceedings* 89(3):374-381.

Tu, H. T., and E. R. Boukus. 2013. *Despite rapid growth, retail clinic use remains modest.* Center for Studying Health System Change.

Urden, L. D. 2002. Patient satisfaction measurement: Current issues and implications. *Outcomes Management* 6(3):125-131.

Uscher-Pines, L., and A. Mehrotra. 2014. Analysis of Teladoc use seems to indicate expanded access to care for patients without prior connection to a provider. *Health Affairs* 33(2):258-264.

VA (Department of Veterans Affairs). 2014a. *Access audit: System-wide review of access.* Washington, DC: U.S. Department of Veterans Affairs.

———. 2014b. *Interim report: Review of patient wait times, scheduling practices, and alleged patient deaths at the Phoenix Health Care System.* Washington, DC: U.S. Department of Veterans Affairs.

———. 2014c. *Pending wait time using create date for new patients and desired date for established patients.* http://www.va.gov/health/docs/pending_access_data_using_cd_and_dd_11202014.pdf (accessed April 27, 2015).

———. 2014d. *Publication of wait-times for the department for the Veterans Choice program.* Federal Register.

———. 2014e. *Review of patient wait times, scheduling practices, and alleged patient deaths at the Phoenix Health Care System.* Washington, DC: Veterans Health Administration Office of Inspector General.

———. 2014f. *Veterans Access, Choice, and Accountability Act of 2014 fact sheet: Choice program and health care collaboration.* Washington, DC: U.S. Department of Veterans Affairs.

———. 2014g. *Veterans Health Administration blueprint for excellence.* Washington, DC: U.S. Department of Veterans Affairs.

———. 2015a. *Patient access data.* http://www.va.gov/health/access-audit.asp (accessed May 1, 2015).

———. 2015b. *Polytrauma/TBI system of care.* http://www.polytrauma.va.gov/system-of-care/care-facilities/index.asp (accessed April 27, 2015).

Valdez, R. S., E. Ramly, and P. F. Brennan. 2010. *Industrial and systems engineering and health care: Critical areas of research—final report.* Rockville, MD: AHRQ.

Varkey, P., M. K. Reller, and R. K. Resar. 2007. Basics of quality improvement in health care. *Mayo Clinic Proceedings* 82(6):735-739.

Waaijer, A., C. Terhaard, H. Dehnad, G.-J. Hordijk, M. S. v. Leeuwen, C. Raaymakers, and J. Lagendijk. 2003. Waiting times for radiotherapy: Consequences of volume increase for the TCP in oropharyngeal carcinoma. *Radiotherapy and Oncology* 66(3):271-276.

Wagner, E. H. 2000. The role of patient care teams in chronic disease management. *BMJ* 320(7234):569-572.

Wang, E. C., M. C. Choe, J. G. Meara, and J. A. Koempel. 2004. Inequality of access to surgical specialty health care: Why children with government-funded insurance have less access than those with private insurance in Southern California. *Pediatrics* 114(5):e584-e590.

Ward, A. C., and D. K. Sobek II. 2014. *Lean product and process development.* Cambridge, MA: Lean Enterprises Institute

Weber, E. J., S. Mason, J. V. Freeman, and J. Coster. 2012. Implications of England's four-hour target for quality of care and resource use in the emergency department. *Annals of Emergency Medicine* 60(6):699-706.

Weiser, T. G., A. B. Haynes, G. Dziekan, W. R. Berry, S. R. Lipsitz, and A. A. Gawande. 2010. Effect of a 19-item surgical safety checklist during urgent operations in a global patient population. *Annals of Surgery* 251(5):976-980.

Weiss, A. P., G. Chang, S. L. Rauch, J. A. Smallwood, M. Schechter, J. Kosowsky, E. Hazen, F. Haimovici, D. F. Gitlin, C. T. Finn, and E. J. Orav. 2012. Patient- and practice-related determinants of emergency department length of stay for patients with psychiatric illness. *Annals of Emergency Medicine* 60(2):162-171.e165.

REFERENCES

Welch, H. G., M. K. Chapko, K. E. James, L. M. Schwartz, and S. Woloshin. 1999. The role of patients and providers in the timing of follow-up visits. Telephone care study group. *Journal of General Internal Medicine* 14(4):223-229.

Womack, J. P., A. P. Byrne, O. J. Flume, G. Kaplan, and J. Toussaint. 2005. *Going Lean in health care*. Cambridge, MA: Institute for Healthcare Improvement.

Yankelovich, D., and D. Meer. 2006. Rediscovering market segmentation. *Harvard Business Review* 84(2):122-131.

Yasaitis, L. C., J. P. Bynum, and J. S. Skinner. 2013. Association between physician supply, local practice norms, and outpatient visit rates. *Medical Care* 51(6):524-531.

Yoon, P., I. Steiner, and G. Reinhardt. 2003. Analysis of factors influencing length of stay in the emergency department. *Canadian Journal of Emergency Medicine* 5(3):155-161.

Young, T. P., and S. I. McClean. 2008. A critical look at Lean thinking in healthcare. *Quality and Safety in Health Care* 17(5):382-386.

Young, T., S. Brailsford, C. Connell, R. Davies, P. Harper, and J. H. Klein. 2004. Using industrial processes to improve patient care. *BMJ* 328(7432):162-164.

Zamosky, L. 2014. What retail clinic growth can teach us about patient demand. Threat or opportunity: Retail clinic popularity is about convenience. *Medical Economics* 91(1):22-24, 29-30.

Appendixes

A Background Papers   107
   Open Access or Advanced Access Scheduling, 108
   Reengineering Flow Through the Primary Care Office, 112
   Reengineering Flow Through the Acute Care Delivery System, 115
   Framework for Active Patient Involvement in Access and
       Scheduling, 118
   References, 121

B IOM Workshops in Brief   123
   Engineering Optimal Health Care Scheduling: Perspectives for the
       Nation, 124
   Engineering Optimal Health Care Scheduling: Perspectives for the
       Veterans Health Administration, 130

C Committee Member Biographies   135

Appendix A

Background Papers

OPEN ACCESS OR ADVANCED ACCESS SCHEDULING
Mark Murray, M.D., M.P.A.
Mark Murray & Associates, LLC

Primary care services form the core of the ambulatory health care system, are in high demand, and are characterized by the most prolonged waits. Access to robust primary care also lies at the heart of effective delivery system reforms, such as with the formation of accountable care organizations (ACOs) and patient-centered medical homes. Current attempts to triage health care appointments based on anticipated patient acuity are unreliable, costly, and operationally difficult. Preferable is the presumption of same-day response to requests, with patient preference serving as the key determinant of the actual timing and nature of care or provision of alternative arrangements. Presented below is one successful method to provide same- or next-day appointments. Although presented in sequence, many of the steps will overlap in practice. Active involvement of patients and their families is an integral part of the design, implementation, and evaluation of this plan.

Actions in Phase One:
Past and Prospective Data Collection

Current visit rate = total number patient visits in the last year ÷ total number of patients

Demand = the number of appointments generated on any given day. This includes appointments made ON today FOR today and appointments made ON today FOR any day in the future.

* If demand is counted only as appointments seen on any given day, it would only equal the number of appointments on the schedule. The demand calculation could then potentially miss any appointments that could not be accommodated and were therefore pushed out to a future day.

Supply (Capacity) = (the number of appointment slots per day for each clinician in a practice) × (the days of work per week by the clinician)

Activity = the daily number of patients who arrive and receive care from a provider

Panel size = the number of patients seen by a physician in the past 12 months

   a. Patients who have seen only one provider for all visits are assigned to that provider.
   b. Patients who have seen more than one provider are assigned to the provider they have seen most often.
   c. The remaining patients who have seen multiple providers the same number of times are assigned to the provider who performed their most recent physical or health check.

Backlog = appointments booked for future dates = previous demand showing as work to be completed in the future.

Actions in Phase Two: Balancing Demand and Capacity

- Determine panel size for the practice and for each provider within the practice, and calculate the unique unduplicated patients seen in the last year. The panel sizes for each provider may be different.
- Determine the practice visit rate using the practice average as well as the individual visit rates. Recognize that the patient visit rate includes visits to the patients' preferred provider in addition to visits to someone else in the practice.
- Develop a spreadsheet that compares *demand* to *capacity* at both the practice and individual practitioner level.
- If the practice balances but the individuals do not, develop a plan to achieve balance by an immediate transfer of patients or a gradual change of patients through natural attrition. The goal is for each provider to be slightly underpaneled to provide some surge capacity and slack.
- If providers are overpaneled (too many patients per provider), use strategies to reduce demand and improve capacity enhancement to achieve a balance before addressing any backlog.
- Start to measure and record daily demand, capacity, and activity.
- Monitor panel size monthly.
- Determine the current third next available appointment (TNA) for the practice and each provider. In the case of an extended TNA, develop a backlog reduction plan.
- Book future appointments for 3 to 4 months in advance only and do not hide demand within a waiting list.
- After initial review of patient panels, restrict the responsibility for shifting patients from one provider to another to a single individual (a "broker"), and keep track of the reasons for change.

Actions in Phase Three: Addressing Backlog

- Measure extent of backlog. This can be done by TNA or by counting the number of prebooked appointments on the schedule. Some of these patients are appropriately prescheduled in the future due to physiology. The backlog is not as bad as count.
- Set a date to start backlog reduction and an expected end date. The end date will be the start date for the new advanced access schedule

template. Backlog reduction is "everybody work," not just provider work—staying late involves everyone.
- Add capacity in the form of more visits per day in order to stop the delay from accumulating and to catch up to the delay.
- During backlog reduction, there will be three queues:
  — A queue for the currently prebooked appointments for the day,
  — A queue for urgent/same-day appointments, and
  — A queue for patients booked into the future, backlog appointments.
- Initially, the urgent slots will fill early and most of the backlog slots will be urgent. With progress toward eliminating the backlog, gradually loosen the criteria for who gets into the backlog slots. At the end of backlog, as evidenced by a significant reduction in TNA, the backlog slots will be filled by traditional types of appointments.
- Once the backlog is gone, eliminate both the urgent slots and the backlog slots and commit to finishing all the work each day.

Actions in Phase Four: Using the New Scheduling Template

- The goal is to see patients on the day they call the office and not schedule the majority of visits into the future.
- Build the new schedule template with a single appointment type, which will involve a significant workflow change. Instead of appointing new patients to the first open slot on any schedule, schedulers will look for the specific designated provider and appoint to that provider.
- Once there is no daily backlog, as evidenced by open slots each day, continue to measure the TNA for the single appointment type.
- Schedule return patients back late in the week and early in the day, when demand is usually lowest. This is load leveling.
- When scheduling return appointments, it is essential to look at the entire schedule to avoid overbooking of any particular day in the future. The goal is to spread out demand from patients who choose a day other than today with prescheduled return visits in order to preserve enough time for expected daily demand.
- Develop contingency plans:
  — Plan for post-vacation and out-of-office recovery. Make a plan for equitable coverage of patients from the absent providers.
  — Develop a plan to manage the end of the day, particularly when the schedule is "full."
  — Develop a safety-recovery plan to determine if a patient needs to be seen immediately. In the absence of urgency, all patients are offered an appointment today. Most are appointed today. Some may be

APPENDIX A

seen immediately. Patients who choose to wait are appointed onto the future schedule.
- Use a care team workload analysis for the entire practice to drive unnecessary work away from providers.
- Demand reduction strategies can help balance an unbalanced equation or can serve to open capacity for new patients entering the practice when supply and demand are balanced. Examples of demand reduction strategies include:
  — Committing to continuity to reduce "system churn"
  — Doing more with each visit
  — Extending visit internals
  — Using the telephone as a means for follow-up
  — Expanding the use of staff for some appointment work
  — Scheduling group visits when appropriate
- Distribute the new patient work only to underpaneled providers. Monitor the over-under panel monthly, and open or close providers to new patients either monthly or weekly.
- Once the practice is in a steady state, new patients are accepted at the same rate that patients graduate from the practice.
- Create a flow map of the patient journey at the encounter, and identify delays between steps. Use office efficiency strategies to improve the flow of work.

REENGINEERING FLOW THROUGH THE PRIMARY CARE OFFICE

Eugene Litvak, Ph.D.
Institute for Healthcare Optimization

The balance of providing timely appointments to patients who need and want them while maintaining a smoothly running practice can be a challenge. Transition is often best accomplished in phases and involves the active participation of all those affected by the change, including patients and families. The following represents one three-phased approach. Phase one focuses on balancing resources and flow of patients with time-sensitive medical complaints with those with elective or scheduled appointments. The main goals of this phase are to improve patient access for those with time-sensitive needs (same-day access and walk-ins) and to decrease the operational chaos that results from competing demands for appointments. The second phase turns attention to the challenge of smoothing elective or scheduled patient flow, such as appointments for yearly physicals, immunizations, or blood pressure checks. The main goals of this phase are to maintain continuity with a specific provider to maximize the quality of care, decrease competition between scheduled and unscheduled appointments, and to enhance office throughput of patients. The third phase aims to optimize capacity in the office to improve quality, safety, and throughput. Using alternative ways of addressing patient concerns, alternative settings of care, and alternative providers when needed creates the opportunity to correct the size of the appointment type and number to better match capacity with demand.

Actions in Phase I

- Separate patients into homogenous groups (i.e., same-day access or walk-ins versus scheduled flows, new patients versus return patients).
or
- Develop and implement a physician-driven urgency classification system for triage based on key patient symptoms.
- Prospectively collect 3 months of data based on the above classification system to accurately determine case mix in terms of urgency.
- Calculate how many appointment slots are needed based on past statistics and staff accordingly.
- Develop and establish standard operating procedures and processes to appropriately accommodate unscheduled and scheduled patients.
- Reduce waiting times for same-day or walk-ins, increase throughput, and decrease overtime for staff by evaluating patient flow through clinic and the involved processes that provide roadblocks.

- Walk-ins and same-days may not always get to see their own doctor. Continuity is not a problem—another set of eyes may be good.
- Implement redesign, and monitor patient flow performance.

Actions in Phase II

- Prospectively collect 3 months of data based on the above classification system to accurately determine case mix in terms of urgency.
- Track cancellations and no-shows.
- Develop a cancellation policy for scheduled appointments and no-shows. Options include
  — Overbooking patient appointments if the number is less than 10 percent. If for a particular weekday, statistics for a single provider reveal that there are two no-shows, then on average, two patients can be overbooked without any risk of overtime.
  — Allow additional overbooking if providers agree to work until all patients are seen.
- Smooth the flow of scheduled patients to decrease the competition from unscheduled office arrival, such as walk-ins and same-day appointments, maximizing the throughput to decrease wait times.
  — Analyze drivers of variability, and identify necessary scheduling changes to achieve schedule smoothing.
  — Increase officewide throughput to achieve consistent nurse-to-patient staffing.
  — Increase patient placement in appropriate areas within the clinic, such as in registration, lab, office, and checkout.
- Phone call data can be used as a means to improve throughput.
  — Determine the distribution of calls for each day and hour of the day.
  — Determine the drivers of call variability.
  — Develop office strategy and resources for answering phone calls to minimize the loss of potential patients.

Actions in Phase III

- Once scheduled demand is smoothed, determine the number of appointment slots needed for same-day, walk-ins, and prescheduled patients.
- Evaluate the role of artificial variability in flow and scheduling bottlenecks to minimize the influence of provider and staff preference on throughput.
- Estimate resources (e.g., providers, staff, rooms, shared equipment) needed for each type of flow to ensure right care.
  — Determine alternative ways of addressing patient concerns (phone call, e-mail, smart phone data, etc.).

- Consider alternative settings of care (group visits, virtual clinician, mobile health unit, etc.).
- Develop alternative providers when needed (office staff for prescription refills, postdischarge follow-up by nurses, scheduler-led triage, managers for billing and insurance triage, etc.).
- If the number of nonclinical calls is negligible, an ad hoc method to address them could be adequate; however, if the number of these calls is significant, carve out a resource with a defined role to provide nonclinical intervention.

• Prospectively collect data based on the above criteria to accurately determine demand.
• Review office capacity scenarios using data, and make necessary changes to better match capacity to demand.

REENGINEERING FLOW THROUGH THE ACUTE CARE DELIVERY SYSTEM

Eugene Litvak, Ph.D.
Institute for Healthcare Optimization

Coordinating the function of the operating room and inpatient units is one of the most challenging tasks in health system reengineering and is perhaps best tackled in stages. Key to the successful design, implementation, and evaluation of these plans is the active participation of patients and families. The following represents one three-phase approach. Phase one focuses on balancing resources and flow of time-sensitive emergent/urgent with elective/scheduled admissions (mostly surgical). The main goals of this phase are to improve patient access and decrease daily operational chaos that results from competing demands. The second phase turns attention to the challenge of smoothing elective/scheduled patient flow (e.g., surgical, catheterization lab, or radiology procedure) to inpatient units. The main goals of this phase are to improve quality and safety of care on corresponding units, decrease competition between scheduled and unscheduled flow on inpatient units, and to enhance elective surgical or medical throughput (or both) depending on the hospital's priorities. The third phase aims to correctly size inpatient units to improve quality, safety, and throughput to alleviate medical ward bottlenecks that can feed back to the operating room. This phase addresses artificial variability in admissions, discharges, and transfers and improves throughput in selected medicine units by ensuring appropriate patient placement and improving the timeliness of admissions, discharges, and transfers out. In doing so, it also creates the opportunity to correctly size medical wards to better match capacity with demand.

Actions in Phase I

- Develop and implement a surgeon-driven urgency classification system that will determine the maximum acceptable wait time for each surgical case.
- Prospectively collect 3 months of data based on the above classification system to accurately determine case mix in terms of urgency.
- Develop and establish standard operating procedures to appropriately accommodate unscheduled and scheduled flows.
- Evaluate and choose from redesign models based on data.
- Implement redesign, and monitor patient flow performance.

Expected Outcomes in Phase I

- Increased surgical throughput.
- Decreased operating room overtime.

- Decreased wait time for urgent/emergent surgeries, and improved compliance with desired maximal acceptable wait times.
- Decreased hospital acute length of stay for urgent/emergent patients
- Improved outcomes for urgent/emergent surgical patients.
- Enabled further operating room efficiency improvement such as on-time starts, lower turnover time, and high-performance teams for elective blocks.
- Improved patient satisfaction relating to decreased elective case delays.
- Improved staff satisfaction and retention.

Actions in Phase II

- Accurately determine your truly elective inpatient admission volume for the selected service(s).
- Collect prospective data if needed.
- Analyze drivers of variability, and identify necessary scheduling changes to achieve schedule smoothing.
- Assess and realign weekend resources as needed.
- Evaluate and choose from redesign models based on collected data.
- Implement smoothing redesign, and monitor patient flow performance.

Expected Outcomes in Phase II

- Increased throughput in smoothed inpatient unit.
- Increased placement of patients in the optimal units with decreased postanesthesia care unit boarding and interunit transfers.
- Higher reliability in nurse-to-patient staffing level leading to lower morbidity and mortality.
- Improved staff satisfaction and decreased use of nursing overtime.
- Quality improvement in terms of decreased readmissions, decreased use of rapid response teams, decreased rate of hospital-acquired infections, and patient safety issues.

Actions in Phase III

- Develop and implement patient-centered admission, discharge, and transfer criteria that will determine what clinical characteristics are necessary for admission to and discharge from the selected unit(s).
- Implement admission, discharge, and transfer criteria; monitor adherence to criteria as well as patient flow performance.
- Prospectively collect data based on the above criteria to accurately determine demand and clinically appropriate length of stay for the selected unit(s).

- Review bed capacity scenarios using data, and make necessary changes to better match capacity to demand.

Expected Outcomes in Phase III

- Increased placement of patients in the optimal units.
- Decreased waits and emergency department boarding.
- Decreased interunit transfers.
- Improved emergency department and inpatient unit staff satisfaction.
- Potential decrease in acute length of stays.
- Quality improvement with decreased readmissions, decreased use of rapid response teams, decreased rate of hospital-acquired infections, and increased patient safety.

FRAMEWORK FOR ACTIVE PATIENT INVOLVEMENT IN ACCESS AND SCHEDULING

James B. Conway, M.S.
Harvard School of Public Health

Core Principles of Patient- and Family-Centered Care

- Dignity and respect: Providers listen and honor patient and family perspectives and choices.
- Information sharing: Providers share complete and unbiased information in ways that are affirming and useful.
- Patient and providers equally participate in care and decision making.
- Patients and providers equally collaborate in policy and program development, implementation, and evaluation, as well as the delivery of care (IPFCC, 2010).

Tenets of a Patient- and Family-Centered Access and Scheduling System

- Patients are the source of control (IOM, 2001).
- Access is defined from the patient perspective.
  - I get information and services that meet my needs, not just a visit, by using a wide range of asynchronous approaches—smart phone apps, e-visits, my home or workplace, and online scheduling.
  - I have access to the right people to match my needs, not just to physicians, but to community health workers, lay care coordinators, interdisciplinary teams, and pharmacists.
- Right care, right place, right time, every time.
  - "I get the care and information I want and need when, where, and how I want and need it"—Donald Berwick, IOM Engineering Optimal Health Care Scheduling: A Public Workshop (2014).
- Waits can contribute to the burden of illness.
- All health systems set the goal of offering an appointment on the day and time the patient choses.
- The system meets the patient where they are:
  - By expanding hours worked per day and number of days worked per week;
  - By addressing cultural and technological competency;
  - By including navigation assistance whenever needed; and
  - By remembering that, for many patients and family members, engagement is therapeutic.
- All health systems set goals of increasing access, supporting care continuum, and reducing time to next appointment.

- As part of future models, the team comes collectively to the patient as opposed to the patient seeking out multiple individuals.
- Engagement is not just looking good but doing good.

Hypothetical Model of Application

1. Questions arise around health and health care:
   — Patient, family, and staff seek counsel when new questions arise or new information is needed.
   — The system for moving forward is understood by all.
2. Collaborative processes are implemented to move forward and to get answers:
   — Focus first and foremost on meeting the needs of the patient: providing the right care, at the right place and the right time, every time.
   — Use a wide range of asynchronous approaches.
   — Ensure access to the right people to match needs.
   — Engage patient and family members in full partnership, with questions prompted, invited, answered, and understood by all.
   — Make a consultant immediately available.
3. Scheduling test, treatment, consult, and so on:
   — Ensure an efficient processes: one person, one call, one time.
   — Offer a wide range of approaches, such as scheduling online, in person, or over the phone, with navigation and other assistance, such as language and access support, when needed.
   — Determine what works best for the patient and family.
   — Seek out and address any special needs and requirements.
   — Prepare in advance, and provide fact sheets.
4. In the interval: focus on questions and preparations:
   — Ensure immediate access to a person 24/7.
   — Solicit and answer questions.
   — Distribute and follow through on preparations.
   — Provide directions.
   — Provide preappointment notifications.
5. Once the appointment is held:
   — Update administrative needs and medication.
   — Ensure that all parties are on time (patient, family, and staff), or are informed if not.
   — Deliver care in appropriate and respectful setting.
   — All parties prepare questions, listen, and respond.
   — Patient choses who is with them.
   — Document in electronic health record (EHR) system.
   — Next visit follow-up before leaving.

6. Follow-up actions taken:
   — Results and follow-up actions are communicated to patient and family members in real time in person, via end-of-visit note, and in patient portal.
   — Results are communicated to care team in real time.
   — Patient and family members are engaged in any revision to care plan.
7. Ongoing care is provided with care team (patient, family, and all staff).

Patient and Family Collaboration in Design and Continuous Improvement of Access and Scheduling Systems

- Overarching principle: Patients and family members collaborate in policy and program development, implementation, and evaluation, as well as in the delivery of care (IOM, 2011).
- Application: This principle is applied in the individual experience of care, in microsystems, in organizations and systems, and in the community.
- Specific to access and scheduling:
  — Design/re-design: Any time groups meet to design or redesign access to and scheduling of care, patients and family representatives are full members of the design team from the beginning through the end of the process.
  — Continuous improvement: The voice of the patient and family is sought as a key collaborator in improvement.
  — Construct design: Embracing application of the findings on high reliability and mindfulness is a helpful illustration (Weick and Sutcliffe, 2001).
  — Transparency of real-time performance is the goal.
  — Improvement practice is grounded in high-reliability principles of mindfulness as explained in Table A-1.

TABLE A-1 Application of Mindfulness to Patient- and Family- (P&F-) Centered Access and Scheduling

Principle	Definition	Applications to Scheduling
Preoccupation with failure	Regarding small, inconsequential errors as a symptom that something is wrong; finding the half-event	Staff asking, P&F reporting, and everyone listening to what P&Fs experienced in access and scheduling or almost experienced.
Sensitivity to operations	Paying attention to what's happening on the front-line	Staff seeks to understand from P&F the gap between system designs on paper versus actual delivered. P&F are probed for their experience as they moved over time and across the continuum.
Reluctance to simplify	Encouraging diversity in experience, perspective, and opinion	Staff measures the effectiveness in meeting what matters most to P&F. Diverse counsel is sought in all system design. "One-size-fits-all" solutions are rejected.
Commitment to resilience	Developing capabilities to detect, contain, and bounce back from events that do occur	There is a commitment to resilience. Whenever things go wrong, P&F are engaged in the solution. All simulations of new processes are conducted in partnership with P&F.
Deference to expertise	Pushing decision making down and around to the person with the most related knowledge and expertise	There is respect for all that the P&F bring as partners in care at every level of the organization.

REFERENCES

IOM (Institute of Medicine). 2001. *Crossing the quality chasm: A new health system for the 21st century.* Washington, DC: National Academy Press.

IOM. 2011. *Patients charting the course: Citizen engagement and the learning health system: Workshop summary.* Washington, DC: The National Academies Press.

IPFCC (Institute for Patient- and Family-Centered Care). 2010. *What are the core concepts of patient- and family-centered care?* http://www.ipfcc.org/faq.html (accessed November 3, 2014).

Weick, K. E., and K. M. Sutcliffe. 2001. *Managing the unexpected: Assuring high performance in an age of complexity.* Hoboken, NJ: Wiley.

Appendix B

IOM Workshops in Brief

WORKSHOP IN BRIEF · JANUARY 2015

For more information, visit www.iom.edu/optimizingscheduling

Engineering Optimal Health Care Scheduling: Perspectives for the Nation— Workshop in Brief

On November 21, 2014, the Institute of Medicine's (IOM's) Committee on Optimizing Scheduling in Health Care convened a public, one-day workshop titled "Engineering Optimal Health Care Scheduling." Funded by the Department of Veterans Affairs (VA), the aim of the session was to explore standards for patient access to health care services across the continuum of care to inform the work of the committee and to shape the content of their upcoming consensus report.

As outlined in introductory comments by committee chair Gary Kaplan, CEO of Virginia Mason Health System, the identification and assessment of best practices and standards for wait times in health care require looking at the entire care delivery system as a single and complex entity with many interrelated and dynamic parts. The workshop convened leading authorities on care delivery, operations management, systems engineering, and patient engagement and satisfaction to

- Better understand the current practices and standards in appointment scheduling and reasons for variation;
- Consider optimization strategies and experiences in health care and other industries;
- Discuss the role of patients and family as catalysts for achieving operational excellence in health care;
- Explore the changing mental model for frontline personnel involved with scheduling improvements; and
- Examine the disciplined structure for change and a strategic and scalable approach to continuous improvement.

The workshop included four panels: current best practices, patient experiences and expectations, technical approaches to wait time improvement, and an overview of the day's discussion. In addition, a working lunch session considered issues in identifying a toolkit for health systems to implement optimal scheduling practices. For each panel, a moderator and several speakers provided framing comments and presentations that then opened to general discussion. This brief summary of the workshop captures the major topics and issues that emerged over the course of the day and is accompanied by a Workshop in Brief specifically targeted to perspectives for the Veterans Health Administration. Statements, recommendations, and opinions expressed are those of individual presenters and participants and are not necessarily endorsed or verified by the Committee on Optimizing Scheduling in Health Care or the IOM, and they should not be construed as reflecting any group consensus.

Current State: Practices, Standards, and Innovation

Throughout the course of the workshop, many presenters and commenters, including Kaplan and Mark Hallett of ThedaCare Center for Healthcare Value, emphasized the importance of addressing this issue from a systems view, focused on the value stream throughout the continuum of care. "Underlying the system changes are the stories that either propel us to new pinnacles or keep us pinned to our current performance," said Peter Pronovost of Johns Hopkins Medicine.

The observation came from many speakers that the components that drive the scheduling process are dynamic and require continuous monitoring and balancing of the supply and demand on the system.

> Our scheduling process actually begins with a single question when we get a patient calling on the phone. That question is: "Would you like to be seen today?" Recognizing that patients have different needs and different behaviors, and in fact, those behaviors, be it speed sensitive or relationship sensitive, aren't static. They are dynamic. They change based on the situation (Hallett).

David Krier of Cincinnati Children's Hospital emphasized in his presentation that "from [Cincinnati Children's] perspective, it is not terribly complicated, but that doesn't mean it is easy . . . For the most part, we have kept our focus on supply. That is primarily because it was within our sphere of control to do so." Terra Thompson, also from Cincinnati Children's Hospital, expanded upon this concept, detailing the processes and measurements that the health system uses to gauge their capacity (see Figure 1, page 3). They have found that making the financial and productivity data available to their providers is key.

Continuing the notion of using a systems approach to improve access and wait times, Andrew Gettinger, of the Office of the National Coordinator for Health IT, stated in his presentation that managing outcomes goes beyond managing IT. He outlined the variation in the scheduling systems at the Dartmouth Hitchcock Hospital and Lahey Clinic, explaining that neither system was better, but rather built to produce outcomes specific to their unique environments. "I don't believe it is about the IT. I believe it is about the operations that implement the IT," he said. Reflecting on the panel, Steven Lawless of Nemours introduced the distinction between designing a system to be optimal versus efficient. "Efficient could be more of an internal phenomenon; optimal has to be from the customer's perspective," said Lawless.

Patients and Families as Change Agents: Experiences and Expectations

The need to engage patients and family members in the beginning stages of designing a better scheduling system was raised by several speakers and discussants, both with respect to improving patient satisfaction in current systems as well as achieving optimal systems in the future. Panelists divided their comments to focus on the human factors aspect of scheduling and the patient perspective on wait times.

Sara Czaja from the University of Miami provided an overview of the changing trends in consumer expectations and roles in their care. Cjaza noted that "consumers are expected to be empowered and take a more active role in health self-management. There is an increased use of technology within the health care arena that has expanded the realm of health-related tasks that consumers are expected to or can perform." Pascale Carayon, University of Wisconsin, continued on this theme, speaking to the multifaceted role of the scheduler. As Carayon put it, "They also have huge social organizational functions. Their role is a lot more than a formal role. There are a lot other informal roles… [and] it is really unclear whether providing different technology is something that is going to reduce or potentially increase visits in the clinic."

David Andrews noted that from his standpoint as a patient with significant experiences with waits and scheduling, "How much of the issue is the wait, [and] how much is the communication about the wait?" He and several other commenters discussed the importance of turning time spent waiting into valuable time in which information is exchanged between the provider and patient. Ashley Benedict of the VA spoke to the potential value that could be added if IT systems could integrate patient appointment times with clinical needs, to identify and complete work that could be done prior to the patient–physician face-to-face.

The discussions of human factors and patient perspective were synthesized into closing remarks by Kristen Carmen of the American Institutes for Research, who noted that "efficiency and optimization is always from a perspective, purchaser's perspective, payer's perspective, patient's perspective, and provider's perspective. I think we need to do a much better job of making those differences in perspective or those commonalities in perspectives transparent."

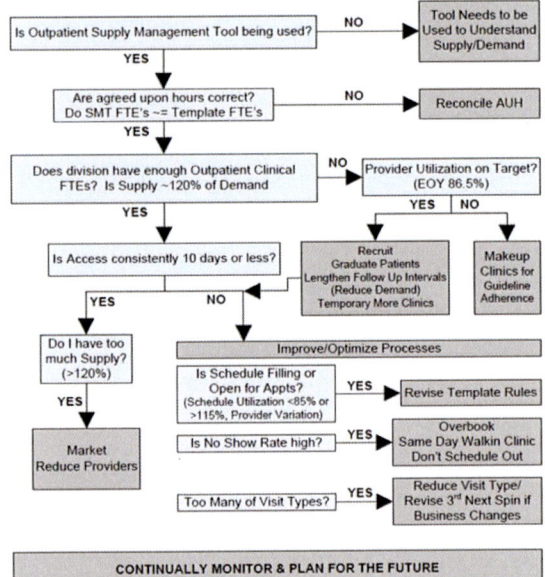

FIGURE 1 Cincinnati Children's Hospital scheduling algorithm to effectively match supply and demand to improve access to care.

NOTES: AUH = agreed-upon hours; EOY = end of year; FTE = full-time equivalent; SMT = supply management tool.

Copies of this document may be distributed to any organization for the global purpose of improving child health. Examples of approved uses of this document include the following:

- copies may be provided to anyone involved in the organization's process for developing and implementing improved scheduling and access
- the model may be adopted or adapted for use within the organization, provided that Cincinnati Children's Hospital Medical Center receives appropriate attribution on all written or electronic documents; and
- copies may be provided to patients and the clinicians who manage their care.

Notification to Cincinnati Children's at childrens-quality@cchmc.org when this document is being adopted, adapted, implemented, or hyperlinked to by your organization is appreciated. © 2014 Cincinnati Children's Hospital Medical Center.

SOURCE: Cincinnati Children's Hospital, as presented by David Krier and Terra Thompson on November 21, 2014.

A Roadmap for the Nation

William Pierskalla of the UCLA Anderson School of Management facilitated a discussion on developing a short-term roadmap for institutions to address scheduling issues and to begin transitioning to an optimal method of scheduling and access to care. He highlighted the major components of the care delivery process: the pre-visit period of scheduling and patient arrival to the care facility, the waiting period prior to connecting with the provider, and the period in which care services are delivered. He emphasized that improving patient flow through these stages required continuous process improvement rather than addressing issues and increasing resources in each discrete period.

To kick off the audience participation portion of the workshop, Pierskalla asked where the roadmap begins. A range of ideas emerged. Both Kaplan and Andrews underscored the need to engage patients at the ground level of transformation. Michael Davies of the VA noted the importance of increased transparency and standardization of acceptable wait times used across the nation, in both public and private sectors. Jackie Griffin of the Department of Defense (DoD) advocated for increased flexibility in hospital operating procedures, and Michael Dinneen of the DoD re-emphasized the need to assess the entire value stream rather than individual parts.

Pierskalla guided the conversation from high-level comments on culture change to focus on the specific measures that health care institutions could implement to affect said change. Several participants considered the incorporation of a measure assessing the linkage between mortality and wait times. Teri Pipe of Arizona State University suggested that measures should focus on the patient and caregiver experience as well as the experiences of inter-professional and interdisciplinary teams in the hospital setting. Patricia Gabow, formerly of Denver Health, described the need to distinguish measures by application, on the individual or system level. Warren Sandberg cautioned against focusing on individual metrics given the complexity of the system, saying that by doing so, "we may actually sub-optimize the system." Kaplan echoed this sentiment and described the approach at Virginia Mason, in which every employee is required to have a comprehensive understanding of the management system and its basic principles.

Technical Approaches to Wait Time Improvement

Thomas Nolan from the Institute for Healthcare Improvement framed the panel by acknowledging that other industries have had success with implementing technical approaches, using "scheduling as an intervention" to optimize customer satisfaction and reduce waste in systems. The presenters used their experiences working both in health care and other industries to detail the ways in which IT tools can be harnessed to implement systems changes to scheduling processes in the care delivery setting.

Wes Walker of Cerner described innovative health IT tools, such as mobile scheduling platforms and patient portals that are being implemented by individual organizations across the country that view access and scheduling improvement as a key component of achieving high-quality care. As he put it, "[The University of Missouri Health System] put the patient at the center, and they looked at the holistic process with the understanding and the idea that the appointment was a means to an end. The goal was the clinical interaction."

Speaking from her expertise in operations research, Zelda Zabinsky of the University of Washington provided several anecdotes of the consequences related to a segmented approach to improving patient flow, thus emphasizing the importance of maintaining a systems view when tackling these issues. Determining the specific bottleneck in the system is difficult, said Zabinsky, describing the phenomenon: "You have a big balloon, and you squeeze one place, and it pops out another place."

Judy Worth, of the Lean Transformations Group, LLC, provided strategies for creating sustainable organizational change across a value stream according to Lean principles (see Figure 2, page 5). Reflecting on the implementation of Lean principles in manufacturing operations, Worth highlighted the need to connect these principles to the institution's broader purpose and goals, as was learned from the Toyota experience.

Several of the discussants raised the issue of an unevenly distributed workflow burden with the implementation of some of these IT tools, and stressed that the tools showing the most promise are those that are collaborative in nature. While agreeing that IT tools are adding value, Michael Harrison, from the Agency for Healthcare Research and Quality, noted, "You can get a really fantastic algorithm that is going to solve a specific problem, but it doesn't generate capacity among the members of that system to deal with the next thing down the line, whether it is an unintended consequence or something else."

1. Pick processes that matter.
2. Start with a win—for the people doing the work.
3. Be clear about scope and don't creep!
4. Get the right people on the bus.
5. Go and see (go to *gemba*).
6. Eat the elephant one bite at a time—but plan to eat it all.
7. Count, count, count—but count the right things!
8. Experiment before you implement.
9. Don't be afraid to take it outside.
10. Make it visual and make it fun—or at least not painful.

FIGURE 2 The Lean Enterprise Institute's 10 Strategies for Organizational Change.
NOTE: Gemba = Japanese word for "the real place."
SOURCE: Judy Worth of the Lean Transformations Group, LLC, as presented on November 21, 2014.

Best Practices for Health Care

Donald Berwick from the Institute for Healthcare Improvement reminded the workshop audience of the charge set by Kaplan at the beginning of the day to inform the committee on the best practices and strategic priorities that could be included in the report recommendations. He opened the final panel with a series of questions: "What did you hear that is cross-cutting and memorable? What are the implications of what we heard today for future steps to take? One of the things I am going to be thinking about and hope our panelists will comment on is: is there any way to accelerate the embrace of the sciences of systems in the kind of care we give?"

Maureen Bisognano of the Institute for Healthcare Improvement re-emphasized the need to redesign the care delivery system around the user, patients and caregivers. Christine Sinsky of the American Medical Association highlighted the discussion points surrounding balancing supply and demand from a systems view. Robert Dittus of Vanderbilt University reviewed the players and resources that health care organizations need in order to fully implement systems engineering methods. He advocated for more coordination among health care teams, and for redefining these teams to include industrial engineers, mathematicians, and most importantly, patients as equal contributors. Additionally, he spoke to the variation across the care continuum and recommended that systems be flexible, saying, "If your scheduling system doesn't acknowledge the different settings that can be utilized, you are not going to have the right system."

Kaplan closed the session by inviting the audience to view the workshop as a call to action. "We need to create a movement," he said. "I think the trump card is really the patients and how we galvanize our communities around what is reasonable to expect from the health care system, and then, how do we make sure that we use the systems engineering approaches as well as the many other things that we have talked about to make that happen."

DISCLAIMER: This workshop in brief has been prepared by **Elizabeth Johnston** and **Katherine Burns,** rapporteurs, as a factual summary of what occurred at the meeting. The statements made are those of the authors or individual meeting participants and do not necessarily represent the views of all meeting participants, the planning committee, or the National Academies.

REVIEWERS: To ensure that it meets institutional standards for quality and objectivity, this workshop in brief was reviewed by **Brian Denton,** University of Michigan; **Michael Dinneen,** U.S. Department of Defense; and **Robert Dittus,** Vanderbilt University Medical Center. **Chelsea Frakes,** Institute of Medicine, served as review coordinator.

SPONSORS: This workshop was supported by the Department of Veterans Affairs/Veterans Health Administration.

For additional information regarding the workshop, visit http://www.iom.edu/optimizingscheduling.

Copyright 2015 by the National Academy of Sciences. All rights reserved.

WORKSHOP IN BRIEF — JANUARY 2015

For more information, visit www.iom.edu/optimizingscheduling

INSTITUTE OF MEDICINE
OF THE NATIONAL ACADEMIES
Advising the nation • Improving health

Engineering Optimal Health Care Scheduling: Perspectives for the Veterans Health Administration— Workshop in Brief

On November 21, 2014, the Institute of Medicine's (IOM's) Committee on Optimizing Scheduling in Health Care convened a public, one-day workshop titled "Engineering Optimal Health Care Scheduling." Funded by the Department of Veterans Affairs (VA), the aim of the session was to explore appropriate standards for access, triage, and scheduling of health care services across the continuum of care to inform the work of the committee and to shape the content of their forthcoming consensus report.

As outlined in introductory comments by committee chair Gary Kaplan, CEO of Virginia Mason Health System, the workshop convened leading authorities on care delivery, operations management, systems engineering, and patient engagement and satisfaction. Kaplan discussed the potential role that systems engineering could play in driving improvement in health care. "How do we better bring together the systems engineering principles that have been so effective in so many industries and yet have gotten only very little traction in health care?" he asked. He said that applying systems thinking and intelligently deploying measurement and analysis could be transformative for the health care system by unlocking new potential pathways for change.

The workshop included four panels: current best practices, patient experiences and expectations, technical approaches to wait time improvement, and an overview of the day's discussion. In addition, a working lunch session considered issues in identifying a toolkit for health systems to implement optimal scheduling practices. For each panel, a moderator and several speakers provided framing comments and presentations that then opened to general discussion.

This brief summary of the workshop captures the major topics and issues discussed over the course of the day that are most applicable to the Veterans Health Administration, and it is accompanied by a Workshop in Brief targeted at perspectives for the broader U.S. health care system. Statements, recommendations, and opinions expressed are those of individual presenters and participants and are not necessarily endorsed or verified by the Committee on Optimizing Scheduling in Health Care or the IOM, and they should not be construed as reflecting any group consensus.

Current VA Practices and Standards in Appointment Scheduling

Peter Pronovost of Johns Hopkins Medicine introduced the session on current practices and standards, saying that the controversy regarding VA wait times for available appointments brought to light needless suffering and the disrespect associated with poor management of scheduling and resources at the VA and in the health care system nationally. This session was an opportunity, he said, to hear stories told by organizations that were able to make meaningful improvements in this area. "Underlying the system changes are the stories that either propel us to new pinnacles or keep us pinned to our current performance," he said.

Throughout the first panel discussion, speakers discussed the challenges, limitations, and opportunities for the VA in its efforts to improve scheduling. Mike Davies of the VA noted that the VA faces a variety of technical challenges. "The VA's information system is 30 years old," he said, and the VA has been asked to measure individual patient waiting times, which is a complex and sophisticated function. David Krier of Cincinnati Children's Hospital noted that the VA currently measures wait times, in the context of an appointment visit cycle time, as the time between when registration ends and when a clinician begins to document in the electronic record. As a result, he said, the VA has not yet been able to monitor how long patients wait in the exam room, or more generally, how much time may be wasted once a clinical encounter begins. He acknowledged that this challenge exists in the private sector as well. "I think that is what our biggest struggle is," said Krier.

Patients and Families as Catalysts for Achieving Operational Excellence in Health Care

The second panel of the day focused on the perspectives, needs, and roles of patients in optimizing scheduling. Matt Puglisi, a veteran now working at Aptima, Inc., provided background on some of the specific challenges the VA faces in meeting patients' expectations for timely care. "The VA system was not consciously designed," he said, instead growing over time, beginning with the Civil War, in reaction to post-war needs for expanded health care resources for veterans. He noted that categorization and associated eligibility requirements for veterans contribute significantly to the complexity of connecting veterans with needed health care services at the VA. "The eligibility for an individual veteran depends. Did you serve during the war? Do you have a service-connected disability? How bad is that disability? That affects what care can be provided by the VA." These decisions about eligibility are further complicated when patients are also eligible for Medicare and/or Medicaid or have private insurance.

Several commenters, including Ashley Benedict from the VA and Pascale Carayon from the University of Wisconsin, also discussed the significance of variations in patients' perceptions of wait times. "The idea of perceived versus actual wait is not the same for every patient," said Benedict. Additionally, Benedict noted a need for balancing measures for people's perceptions. "From the IT component, if we could predict what patients needed and their appointments coming up, and I could get my lab work done, that might not be a waiting time for me because there is a value-added activity that is happening between now and being seen in my actual appointment." Carayon and Puglisi discussed some of the potential limitations of measuring time alone in assessing waits, noting that measures of perceived wait times or of patients' satisfaction with wait times could add critical additional meaning. "You may find that by talking a little to patients if you can spare the time, they may be able to withstand longer wait times and be as or more satisfied," said Puglisi.

Optimization Strategies and Experiences in Health Care

Mark Hallett from ThedaCare Center for Healthcare Value discussed patient-centered scheduling and the practices to improve capacity of their system:

> Our scheduling process actually begins with a single question when we get a patient calling on the phone. That question is: "Would you like to be seen today?" Recognizing that patients have different needs and different behaviors, and in fact, those behaviors, be it speed sensitive or relationship sensitive, aren't static. They are dynamic.

The presenters from Cincinnati Children's Hospital, Krier and Terra Thompson, acknowledged the similarities between their home organization and that of Hallett's as adopters of systems-thinking to transform their systems and achieve high quality results. Yet they also cautioned that even once a system is optimized and performing at its peak capacity, it is still extremely complex and fragile and thus challenging to sustain. As a strategy for maintaining performance, Thompson highlighted the importance of leadership at various levels, stating the need to ensure that clinical leadership at the division level is engaged and aware of their role in the optimization strategies for the system (see Figure 1).

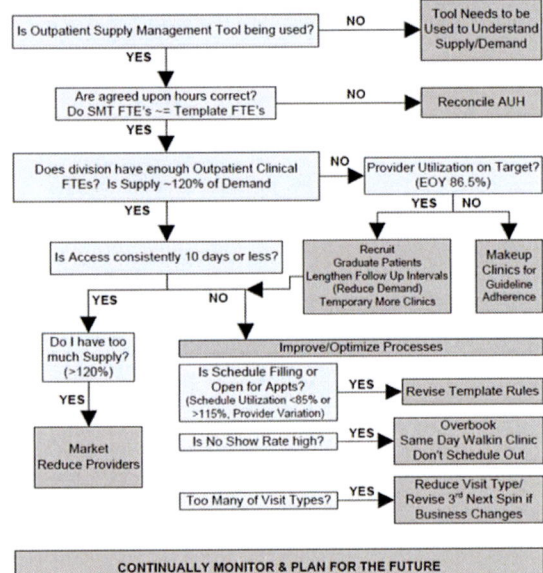

FIGURE 1 Cincinnati Children's Hospital scheduling algorithm to effectively match supply and demand to improve access to care.

NOTES: AUH = agreed-upon hours; EOY = end of year; FTE = full-time equivalent; SMT = supply management tool.

Copies of this document may be distributed to any organization for the global purpose of improving child health. Examples of approved uses of this document include the following:

- copies may be provided to anyone involved in the organization's process for developing and implementing improved scheduling and access
- the model may be adopted or adapted for use within the organization, provided that Cincinnati Children's Hospital Medical Center receives appropriate attribution on all written or electronic documents; and
- copies may be provided to patients and the clinicians who manage their care.

Notification to Cincinnati Children's at childrens-quality@cchmc.org when this document is being adopted, adapted, implemented, or hyperlinked to by your organization is appreciated. © 2014 Cincinnati Children's Hospital Medical Center.

SOURCE: Cincinnati Children's Hospital, as presented by David Krier and Terra Thompson on November 21, 2014.

Several speakers and commenters, including Patty Gabow (Denver Health), Krier, and Hallett, also discussed centralized scheduling as a necessary precondition for achieving a meaningful reduction in wait times, while ensuring that high-quality clinical decision making is applied in triage. Krier said that he would support separating scheduling and triage functions, such that scheduling becomes centralized and triage functions move closer to clinicians.

Andrew Gettinger of the Office of the National Coordinator for Health IT spoke of the operational details that contribute to optimizing scheduling, such as open access to appointment times and appointment pre-approvals. In discussing the ability to enhance capacity using advanced IT tools, such as virtual visits, Christine Sinsky of the American Medical Association cautioned that "they are an enhancement, but they are not necessarily the solution."

Identifying a Structure for Change

In the closing session on common themes and best practices, participants including Davies, Pronovost, and Donald Berwick, Institute for Healthcare Improvement, commented on potential approaches to both improving scheduling at the VA and ensuring that scheduling is well managed throughout the care system. Berwick identified "two different voices in the room"—(1) the conversation focused specifically on the challenges surrounding scheduling mechanics and immediate strategies for improvement, and (2) the conversation focused on broader organizational changes possible by implementing and embracing systems engineering techniques.

Davies and Berwick discussed the potential benefits of identifying baselines and benchmarks for scheduling and wait-time performance, as a tool for both understanding the causes and consequences of wait times and for monitoring progress as interventions are undertaken at the VA. Davies said:

> In the context of all of these forward thinking, clearly exciting and relevant comments, I would just ask you to think about the question of how do we ensure some floor, some standards, something that is a little deeper that would have given us some predictive [indicator] that this was going to happen.

Several discussants, including Benedict and Robert Dittus, Vanderbilt University, emphasized the importance of ensuring that systems engineering approaches are incorporated into the care delivery setting. Kaplan closed the session by reminding the audience that this issue is a national challenge. "We need to create a movement," he said. "I think the trump card is really the patients and how we galvanize our communities around what is reasonable to expect from the health care system, and then, how do we make sure that we use the systems engineering approaches as well as the many other things that we have talked about to make that happen."

DISCLAIMER: This workshop in brief has been prepared by **Katherine Burns, Elizabeth Johnston,** and **Elizabeth Malphrus,** rapporteurs, as a factual summary of what occurred at the meeting. The statements made are those of the authors or individual meeting participants and do not necessarily represent the views of all meeting participants, the planning committee, or the National Academies.

REVIEWERS: To ensure that it meets institutional standards for quality and objectivity, this workshop in brief was reviewed by **Mark Hallett,** ThedaCare; **Christine Sinsky,** American Medical Association; **William W. Stead,** Vanderbilt University; and **Catherine Tantau,** Tantau & Associates. **Chelsea Frakes,** Institute of Medicine, served as review coordinator.

SPONSORS: This workshop was supported by the Department of Veterans Affairs/Veterans Health Administration.

For additional information regarding the workshop, visit http://www.iom.edu/optimizingscheduling.

Copyright 2015 by the National Academy of Sciences.

Appendix C

Committee Member Biographies

Gary Kaplan, M.D., FACP, FACMPE (*Chair*), has served as Chairman and CEO of the Virginia Mason Health System since 2000. He is also a practicing internal medicine physician at Virginia Mason. Dr. Kaplan received his medical degree from the University of Michigan and is board certified in internal medicine. Since Dr. Kaplan became Chairman and CEO, Virginia Mason has received significant national and international recognition for its efforts to transform health care. The Leapfrog Group named Virginia Mason "Top Hospital of The Decade" for patient safety and quality, a distinction shared with only one other hospital. For the fifth consecutive year, The Leapfrog Group also named Virginia Mason as 1 of 65 U.S. hospitals to be designated as a "Top Hospital." In addition, Virginia Mason has received HealthGrades' "Distinguished Hospital Award for Clinical Excellence" for 5 consecutive years. Virginia Mason is considered to be the national leader in deploying the Toyota Production System to health care management. In addition to his patient-care duties and position as CEO, Dr. Kaplan is a clinical professor at the University of Washington and has been recognized for his service and contribution to many regional and national boards, including the Institute for Healthcare Improvement, the Medical Group Management Association, the National Patient Safety Foundation, the Greater Seattle Chamber of Commerce, and the Washington Healthcare Forum. Dr. Kaplan is a founding member of Health CEOs for Health Reform. In 2007, Dr. Kaplan was designated a fellow in the American College of Physician Executives. In 2011, he was named the 12th most influential U.S. physician leader in health care by *Modern Healthcare* magazine, and the same publication ranked Dr. Kaplan 33rd on its list of the "100 Most

Influential People in Healthcare." In 2012, he was named the second most influential U.S. physician leader in health care by the same publication. In 2009, Dr. Kaplan received the John M. Eisenberg Award from the National Quality Forum and The Joint Commission for Individual Achievement at the national level for his outstanding work and commitment to patient safety and quality. Additionally, he was recognized by the Medical Group Management Association (MGMA) as the recipient of the Harry J. Harwick Lifetime Achievement Award. Each year, the MGMA and the American College of Medical Practice Executives honor one individual who has made outstanding nationally recognized contributions to health care administration, delivery, and education in his or her career, advancing the field of medical practice management.

Jana Bazzoli, M.B.A., M.S.A., CMPE, joined the Cincinnati Children's Research Foundation and the Department of Pediatrics as vice president of Clinical Affairs. Ms. Bazzoli has nearly 20 years' experience in hospital administration, having earned her M.B.A. at Augusta State University in Georgia and her M.S.A. at Central Michigan University. Her most recent position was associate administrator of outpatient operations at Nemours/Alfred I. DuPont Hospital for Children in Wilmington, Delaware. At Cincinnati Children's, Ms. Bazzoli works closely with departmental business directors and division directors to improve clinical care and systems. One of her primary responsibilities is to develop and implement new initiatives to achieve the departments' clinical, operational, and academic goals while maintaining Cincinnati Children's quality of care.

James C. Benneyan, Ph.D., is a leading authority on health care systems engineering, founding director of two federally awarded health care engineering centers, and professor of Industrial Engineering and Operations Research at Northeastern University. Dr. Benneyan has served as director, codirector, principal investigator, or co–private investigator in seven engineering research centers, and research laboratories totaling more than $32 million in funding. His research focuses on mathematical modeling and optimization of health care systems broadly, with particular emphasis and area expertise in patient safety, access, logistics, comparative effectiveness, quality, and treatment optimization. Dr. Benneyan currently serves as a director of the National Science Foundation (NSF) Center for Organization Transformation, the New England U.S. Department of Veterans Affairs (VA) Engineering Resource Center, and Northeastern's Quality and Productivity research laboratory. The work of these three enterprises collectively integrates academic research, real-world application, and workforce development. Methods research foci include statistical quality engineering, probabilistic optimization, computer simulation, risk-adjusted statistical methods, rare events, spatial surveillance, risk-benefit, and comparative effectiveness models. Benneyan has published more than 100 papers and served as senior or associate editor of 4 academic journals in the above areas, has received 6 teaching, service, and research awards, and has taught engineering to ages 6 through 60. Dr. Benneyan is a vice president of the Institute for Industrial Engineers (IIE), past president of the Society for Health Systems (SHS), senior fellow and faculty at the Institute for Healthcare Improvement, fellow of SHS and the Healthcare Information and Management Systems Society (HIMSS), operations research faculty for Northeastern's NSF-Nanoscale Science and Engineering Center, Center for High-Rate Nanomanufacturing (CHN), and board member or advisor for several health care organizations. Prior to joining Northeastern, Dr. Benneyan was senior systems engineer for Harvard Community Health Plan, principal of Productivity Sciences Incorporated, and an industrial engineer at IBM and later Digital Equipment Corporation. Primary funding sources include NSF, National Institutes of Health, Veterans Health Administration, National Institute on Drug Abuse, Regenstreif Institute, United Network for Organ Sharing, U.S. Air Force Surgeon General's Office, and Agency for Healthcare Research and Quality.

James Conway, M.S., is an adjunct lecturer at the Harvard School of Public Health in Boston and Senior Consultant for Safe and Reliable Healthcare in Evergreen, Colorado. From 2006 to 2009 he was Senior Vice President of the Institute for Healthcare Improvement (IHI) and from 2005 to 2011, Senior Fellow. During 1995-2005, Mr. Conway was Executive Vice President and Chief Operating Officer of Dana-Farber Cancer Institute, Boston. Prior to joining DFCI, he had a 27-year career at Children's Hospital, Boston, in Radiology Administration, Finance, and as Assistant Hospital Director. His areas of expertise and interest include governance and executive leadership, patient safety, change management, crisis management, and patient- and family-centered care. He holds a Master of Science degree from Lesley College, Cambridge, Massachusetts. Mr. Conway is the winner of numerous awards, including the 1999 ACHE Mass. Regents Award, the 2001 first Individual Leadership Award in Patient Safety by The Joint Commission and the National Committee for Quality Assurance. In 2008, he received the Picker Award for Excellence in the Advancement of Patient Centered Care, in 2009 the Mary Davis Barber Heart of Hospice Award from the Massachusetts Hospice and Palliative Care Federation, and in 2012 both the Institute for Patient and Family Centered Care Leadership Award and the first Honorary Fellowship of the National Association for Healthcare Quality. A Lifetime Fellow of the American College of Healthcare Executives, he has served as a Distinguished Advisor to the Lucian Leape Institute for the National Patient Safety Foundation. Institute of Medicine (IOM) committees have included Identifying and Preventing Medication Errors and a Learning Healthcare System. Current board service includes board member Winchester Hospital; board member American Cancer Society, New England Region; and member, Board of Visitors, University of Massachusetts, Boston. In government service, he served from 2006 to 2010 as a member of the Commonwealth of Massachusetts Quality and Cost Council.

Susan Dentzer is Senior Policy Adviser to the Robert Wood Johnson Foundation, the nation's largest philanthropy focused on health and health care in the United States. In this role, she works closely with foundation leaders to carry out the organizational mission of building a culture of health and improving the health and health care of all Americans. One of the nation's most respected health and health policy thought leaders and journalists, she is also an on-air analyst on health issues on the PBS *NewsHour*. From 2008 to April 2013, she was the editor-in-chief of *Health Affairs*, the nation's leading peer-reviewed journal of health policy, and led the transformation of that journal from a bimonthly academic publication into a highly topical monthly publication and website with more than 120 million page views annually. From 1998 to 2008, she led the PBS *NewsHour*'s health unit as on-air health correspondent and was the recipient of numerous honors and awards. Ms. Dentzer is an elected member of the Institute of Medicine and the Council on Foreign Relations. Ms. Dentzer graduated from Dartmouth College, is a trustee emerita of the college, and chaired the Dartmouth Board of Trustees from 2001 to 2004. She is a member of the Board of Overseers of Dartmouth Medical School and is a member of the board of directors of the International Rescue Committee, a leading humanitarian organization. She is also on the board of directors of Research!America, an alliance working to make research to improve health a higher priority; is a public member of the Board of Directors of the American Board of Medical Specialties; and is a member of the board of directors of the Health Data Consortium, which seeks to foster use of public and private data to improve the health and health care of Americans. A widely admired communicator, Ms. Dentzer is a frequent speaker before a wide variety of health care and other groups and a frequent commentator on such National Public Radio shows such as the *Diane Rehm Show* and *This Life*.

Eva Lee, Ph.D., is a professor in the H. Milton Stewart School of Industrial and Systems Engineering at Georgia Institute of Technology, and Director of the Center for Operations Research in Medicine and HealthCare, a center established through funds from the National Science Foundation (NSF) and the Whitaker Foundation. The center focuses on biomedicine, public health, and defense, advancing domains from basic science to translational medical research; intelligent, quality, and cost-effective delivery;

and medical preparedness and protection of critical infrastructures. She is a Distinguished Scholar in Health Systems, Health System Institute at Georgia Tech and Emory University. She is also co-director of the Center for Health Organization Transformation, an NSF Industry/University Cooperative Research Center. Dr. Lee partners with hospital leaders to develop novel transformational strategies in delivery, quality, safety, operations efficiency, information management, change management, and organizational learning. Dr. Lee's research focuses on mathematical programming, information technology, and computational algorithms for risk assessment, decision making, predictive analytics and knowledge discovery, and systems optimization. She has made major contributions in advances to medical care and procedures, emergency response and medical preparedness, health care operations, and business intelligence and operations transformation. Dr. Lee received the NSF Faculty Early Career Development (CAREER) program Young Investigator Award for research on optimization and parallel algorithms and their applications to large-scale logistics and medical applications. She is the first and only industrial engineer/operations research recipient for the prestigious Whitaker Foundation Biomedical Grant for Young Investigators. In 2005, she received the Institute for Operations Research and Management Sciences Pierskalla Best Paper Award for research excellence in HealthCare Management Science for her work on emergency response and planning, large-scale prophylaxis dispensing, and resource allocation for bioterrorism and infectious disease outbreaks. Together with Dr. Marco Zaider from Memorial Sloan Kettering Cancer Center, they were named winners of the 2007 Franz Edelman award for their work on using operations research to advance cancer therapeutics. Dr. Lee was selected by the National Academy of Engineering (NAE) to serve on the organizing committee and to lead the "Engineering the Healthcare Delivery System" cluster for the 2009 NAE Frontiers of Engineering Symposium for outstanding young engineers. In 2011, her work with the Centers for Disease Control and Prevention on emergency response and mass dispensing was selected as an Edelman finalist. In the same year, her paper on vaccine response immunogenicity prediction in *Nature Immunology* was named "Paper of the Year" by the International Vaccine Society. Her work on optimizing and transforming emergency department workflow and patient care was recognized as second prize winner in the 2013 Daniel H. Wagner Prize Excellence in Operations Research Application. She has received seven patents on innovative medical systems and devices.

Eugene Litvak, Ph.D., is President and CEO of the Institute for Healthcare Optimization (IHO). He is also an Adjunct Professor in Operations Management in the Department of Health Policy & Management at the Harvard School of Public Health, where he teaches the course "Operations Management in Service Delivery Organizations." Since 1995 he has been leading the development and practical application of the innovative Variability Methodology for cost reduction and quality improvement in health care delivery systems. Application of this methodology has resulted in significant quality improvement and multimillion dollar margin improvements for every hospital that has applied it. Dr. Litvak was a member of the Institute of Medicine committees on The Future of Emergency Care in the United States Health System and The Learning Healthcare System in America, as well as a member of the National Advisory Committee to the American Hospital Association for Improving Quality, Patient Safety and Performance. On behalf of IHO, he serves as principal investigator in many hospital operations improvement projects in the United States and internationally, including the Centers for Medicare & Medicaid Services–funded Partnership for Patients initiative with 14 hospitals in New Jersey and the nationwide Whole System Patient Flow Improvement initiative in Scotland.

Mark Murray, M.D., is an international authority on the development of access and flow systems within health care. He has specific expertise in areas such as patient access to appointments in primary, specialty, and ancillary care; patient access to information; and health care demand/supply matching and balance. Drawing from his direct experience in health care delivery and management, Dr. Murray has a unique perspective as a physician who practiced in multiple environments, as well as an understanding of how other businesses and industries use flow and demand/supply matching. He has also initiated and developed multioperational quality improvement efforts and has consulted with health care organizations worldwide on a variety of quality improvement strategies, including efficiencies in office practices, the development of health care teams, change management in health care settings, physician compensation, and "big system" flow. Dr. Murray has worked with various types of organizations, including the U.S. government; fee-for-service and capitated environments; health practices, systems, plans, and organizations; insurance companies; and various medical groups. In addition, he has worked extensively abroad. Dr. Murray completed his undergraduate training at St. Mary's College in California; attended Creighton University Medical School in Omaha, Nebraska; completed a residency in Family Medicine at the University of California, Davis; and obtained a master's degree in Health Services Administration from St. Mary's College. Following his medical training, he organized and developed a medical practice in an underserved rural area in Northern California. He also worked for Kaiser Permanente for 19 years, holding various administrative positions, including Assistant Chief of Medicine, North Sacramento Valley, where he had operational responsibility for the care of 270,000 patients; and director of a regional call center that served 1.2 million patients. He left Kaiser in 1999 to pursue independent consulting on waits and delays in health care.

Thomas Nolan, Ph.D., is a statistician, author, and member of Associates in Process Improvement, a group that specializes in the improvement of quality and productivity. Over the past 25 years, he has assisted organizations in many different industries in the United States, Canada, and Europe. He is a Senior Fellow of the Institute for Healthcare Improvement (IHI). At IHI he has guided the Research and Development function and led several of IHI's strategic international initiatives such as the Triple Aim. His health care experience includes helping integrated systems, hospitals, and medical practices to accelerate the improvement of quality and the reduction of costs in clinical and administrative services. Dr. Nolan holds a doctorate in statistics from George Washington University and is the author of three books on improving quality and productivity. He has published articles on quality and safety in a variety of peer-reviewed journals, including the *Journal of the American Medical Association* and the *British Medical Journal*. He was the year 2000 recipient of the Deming Medal awarded by the American Society for Quality. In 2010 the Statistics Division of the American Society for Quality awarded him the William Hunter Award for innovative applications of statistical methods.

Peter Pronovost, M.D., Ph.D., is a practicing anesthesiologist and critical care physician who is dedicated to finding ways to make hospitals and health care safer for patients. In June 2011, he was named director of the new Armstrong Institute for Patient Safety and Quality at Johns Hopkins, as well as Johns Hopkins Medicine's senior vice president for patient safety and quality. Dr. Pronovost has developed a scientifically proven method for reducing the deadly infections associated with central-line catheters. His simple but effective checklist protocol virtually eliminated these infections across the state of Michigan, saving 1,500 lives and $100 million annually. These results have been sustained for more than 3 years. Moreover, the checklist protocol is now being implemented across the United States, state by state, and in several other countries. *The New Yorker* magazine says that Dr. Pronovost's "work has already saved more lives than that of any laboratory scientist in the past decade." Dr. Pronovost has chronicled his work to improve patient safety in his book, *Safe Patients, Smart Hospitals: How One Doctor's Checklist Can Help Us Change Health Care from the Inside Out*. In addition, he has written more than 400 articles and chapters related to patient safety and the measurement and evaluation of safety efforts. He serves in an advisory capacity to the World Health Organization's World Alliance for Patient Safety. Dr. Pronovost has earned several national awards, including the 2004 John Eisenberg Patient Safety

Research Award and a coveted MacArthur Fellowship in 2008, known popularly as the "genius grant." He was named by *Time* magazine as 1 of the world's 100 "most influential people" for his work in patient safety. He regularly addresses Congress on the importance of patient safety, prompting a report by the U.S. House of Representatives' Committee on Oversight and Government Reform strongly endorsing his intensive care unit infection prevention program. Dr. Pronovost previously headed Johns Hopkins' Quality and Safety Research Group and was medical director of Hopkins' Center for Innovation in Quality Patient Care. Both groups, as well as other partners throughout the university and health system, have been folded into the Armstrong Institute.

Ronald M. Wyatt, M.D., is the medical director in the Division of Healthcare Improvement at The Joint Commission. In this role, Dr. Wyatt promotes quality improvement and patient safety to internal and external audiences, works to influence public policy and legislation for patient safety improvements, and serves as the lead patient safety information and education resource within The Joint Commission. Dr. Wyatt collaborates in the development of National Patient Safety Goals, and oversees data management and analyses related to the Sentinel Event database. Prior to coming to The Joint Commission, Dr. Wyatt served as the director of the Patient Safety Analysis Center at the Department of Defense (DoD) where he directed and maintained the DoD Patient Safety Registries. These registries house de-identified clinical, root cause analyses, and failure mode and effects analyses data on the DoD's adverse patient safety events. Previously, Dr. Wyatt was the medical director at several health care organizations where his responsibilities included directing patient safety and quality improvement activities. He also served as a captain in the U.S. Army Reserves and was on active duty in the Internal Medicine Clinic at Reynolds Army Hospital in Ft. Sill, Oklahoma. He has received numerous awards, including a U.S. Army Commendation Medal for his service in Desert Storm. Dr. Wyatt served on the Food and Drug Administration (FDA) Drug Safety Oversight Board, the Agency for Healthcare Research and Quality (AHRQ) Science of Public Reporting Special Emphasis Panel, and the Comprehensive Unit-Based Safety Program to Eliminate Health Care–Associated Infections (CUSP) Technical Expert Panel. He is a mentor to the Center for Medicare & Medicaid Innovation (CMI) Advisors program at the Centers for Medicare & Medicaid Services (CMS) and a member of the American College of Physicians. Dr. Wyatt is on the faculty at the Institute for Health Care Improvement. He was named 1 of the "Top 50 Patient Safety Experts" in the United States by *Becker's* magazine in 2013 and 2014. Areas of special interests include social determinants of health, health disparity, patient activation, and professionalism (disruptive behavior). Dr. Wyatt co-authored the DoD

Patient Activation tool kit. He contributed to the National Patient Safety Goal on Medical Alarm Management, the revised Sentinel Event Policy, and the development and writing of the Patient Safety Systems chapter for The Joint Commission hospital accreditation manual. Dr. Wyatt is an internist with more than 20 years of practice experience and is currently licensed in the state of Alabama. He earned his medical degree at the University of Alabama at Birmingham and completed residency at the St. Louis University hospital, where he served as the first African-American Chief Resident in the department of Internal Medicine. Dr. Wyatt earned the Executive Master of Science in Health Administration (MSHA) from the University of Alabama at Birmingham. In 2000, the Morehouse School of Medicine conferred Dr. Wyatt with an honorary Doctor of Medical Sciences degree. As a George W. Merck Fellow with the Institute for Healthcare Improvement in 2009-2010, Dr. Wyatt was trained in performance improvement, measurement, epidemiological, and statistical principles. He also completed a Harvard School of Public Health program in Clinical Effectiveness—a joint program of Brigham and Women's Hospital, Massachusetts General Hospital, Harvard Medical School, and Harvard School of Public Health. Dr. Wyatt actively presents on a variety of patient safety topics throughout the United States and Canada. He has written and published numerous articles on patient safety topics.